ISRAEL

ONE LAND, TWO PEOPLES

ISRAEL

ONE LAND, TWO PEOPLES

Harry B. Ellis

Thomas Y. Crowell Company, New York

The Dome of the Rock on the Temple Mount in Old
Jerusalem is a sacred Moslem and Jewish site. Here
tradition says Abraham bound Isaac for sacrifice
to the Lord, and Mohammed ascended to heaven.
(Israel Government Tourist Office)

By the Author

ISRAEL: *One Land, Two Peoples*

IDEALS AND IDEOLOGIES: *Communism,
    Socialism, and Capitalism*

THE COMMON MARKET

THE ARABS

CHALLENGE IN THE MIDDLE EAST

ISRAEL AND THE MIDDLE EAST

HERITAGE OF THE DESERT: *The Arabs and the Middle East*

Maps by Walter Hortens

Copyright © 1972 by Harry B. Ellis

Designed by Abigail Moseley

Manufactured in the United States of America

L. C. Card 73-175104
ISBN 0-690-45028-1

1 2 3 4 5 6 7 8 9 10

To Andrew

Contents

1   Two Palestinian Villages   1

2   The Sons of Abraham   13

3   Zionism and the Exiled Jews   25

4   Palestine Under Mandate   43

5   Three Arab-Jewish Wars   61

6   Israel and the Arabs   79

7   Who Is a Jew?   105

8   Guns, Butter, and Taxes   121

9   Politics in Israel   133

10   The United States and Israel   149

11   The Morality of the Case   167

    Books for Further Reading   174

    Index   177

1

Two Palestinian Villages

The ancient Hebrews, struggling toward the promised land, were told by their prophets that Palestine flowed with milk and honey. In fact, however, Palestine is one of the least endowed lands on earth. Much of it is desert and rugged, arid hills, and only the utmost in human endeavor has subdued the land and made the desert bloom.

There is, in other words, little in the harsh geography of Palestine to explain the veneration felt for it by millions of Christians, Jews, and Moslems throughout the world. Palestine is a small country, a little larger than Connecticut, about one-fourth the size of New York State. To the west, Palestine is bounded by the Sinai Peninsula, the United Arab Republic, and the Mediterranean Sea. North of Palestine lie Lebanon and Syria. To the east lies the Arab kingdom of Jordan and the border area formed by the great rift, or valley, through which flows the Jordan River. The southern tip of Palestine probes the clear blue waters of the Gulf of Aqaba.

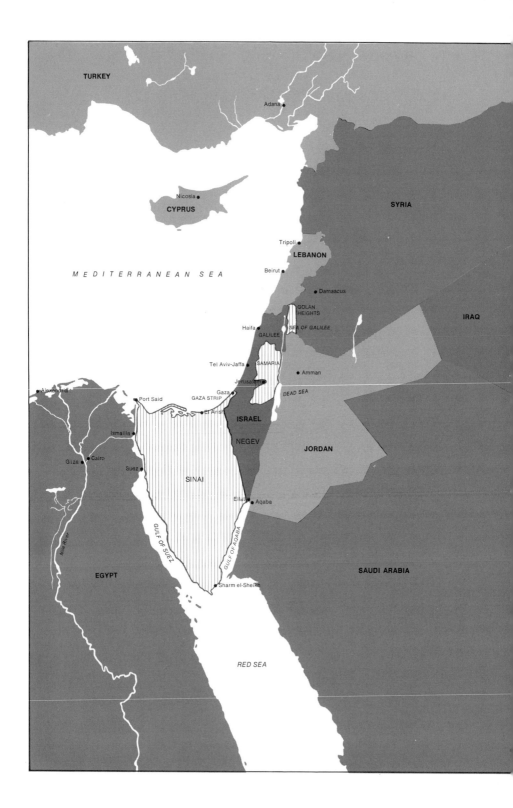

A road descending to the Dead Sea in the wilderness of the Negev desert.

There is a triangle of parched desert in the south, the wilderness of the Negev, broken by stark escarpments of sandstone hills which glow mauve, pink, and brown in the light of the setting sun, but are devoid of green growth. This wilderness ends in the north at the Dead Sea, a lake so salt that life cannot exist in its waters. The Dead Sea is the lowest spot on earth, 1,286 feet below sea level.

Here, on the western shore of this bitter lake, stood biblical Sodom and Gomorrah, and here Lot's wife was said to have become a pillar of salt when she turned to watch God raining "fire and brimstone" on the sinful cities.

Straight north of the Dead Sea runs the Jordan River valley, also barren except for scattered oases, of which Jericho is the best known. West of the Jordan River rise the rugged Judean Mountains, crowned by the city of Jerusalem. Farther north these heights become gentler and are called the hills of Samaria.

On the western slope of these Judean and Samarian heights lies a fertile coastal plain, in some places less than ten miles wide. This plain, nourished by winter rains and by water pumped through pipelines from the Jordan River, is the heart-

The partially reconstructed ruins of the ancient city of Avdat are a major point of interest in Israel's Negev desert. (Israel Government Tourist Office)

Tel Aviv, on the Mediterranean shore, seen from the bell tower of St. Peter's Church in Jaffa. (Israel Government Tourist Office)

land of the modern State of Israel. Here live most of the nation's people. Here also are Israel's two largest cities, Tel Aviv and Haifa. Oranges, lemons, strawberries, and other fruits and vegetables grown on this sunny plain find their way to market shelves throughout Europe, as do fresh-cut flowers, flown daily by Israeli exporters to florists in many European lands.

Fifty-five miles north of Tel Aviv, Mount Carmel curves down to the sea and the coastal plain ends abruptly. North of Mount Carmel, where the Bible says that the Hebrew prophet Elijah called down the fire of God to confound the disciples of Baal, is the Bay of Acre. Along the shores of this quiet bay, beneath the looming ruins of ancient Crusader battlements, Arab fishing boats are drawn up in colorful array.

A sidewalk cafe in Tel Aviv.

Just north of Carmel an east-west flatland, called the Plain of Esdraelon, cuts through the hills. Beyond Esdraelon the gray mountains of Galilee tumble northward to the frontier of Lebanon. Nazareth, early home of Jesus and today the largest Arab city in the Jewish State of Israel, spans a valley in the Galilean hills.

This, then, is the geography of Palestine—a desert wilderness in the south, a backbone ridge of mountains running north-south through the country, the Jordan River valley to the east, and a fertile coastal plain fronting the Mediterranean Sea.

What the Holy Land means to people who live there came clear to me during visits at varying times to two Palestinian villages—an Arab town named Qalqilya and an Israeli settlement called Nir Eliahu. The farmers of Qalqilya had built their houses of mud or cut stone against the lower slopes of the brown Samarian hills, leaving free the coastal plain which stretched between the town and the Mediterranean Sea. Here, on this rich plain, lay the wealth of Qalqilya—acres of orange groves and wheat fields.

The fruit and grain of these fields found ready markets, inside and outside Palestine, and made Qalqilya a prosperous town. Then came the Arab-Jewish war of 1948, resulting in the creation of the State of Israel. When the guns fell silent early in 1949, armistice lines between Arabs and Jews were drawn where the contending armies stood. As it happened, Jewish forces had occupied the coastal plain but not the houses of Qalqilya itself. Thus the town remained in the Arab kingdom of Jordan, while the fields which supported it were awarded to Israel.

View of the city of Haifa, Israel's northern harbor. Across the bay is the old city of Acre.

Overnight the farmers of Qalqilya were cut off from their means of livelihood. They still had their homes, but not their groves and fields. When I first visited Qalqilya in 1953, the mayor and I climbed the tall minaret of the mosque in the center of town. Below us, like sheep around their shepherd, clustered the roofs of Qalqilya. Just beyond the buildings of the town ran a line of white pillars, marking the frontier. Then came the coastal plain, busy that day with the noise and dust of Israeli tractors, cultivating fields which the Arabs of Qalqilya regarded as their own.

"There," declared the mayor, pointing to a field where a pump spurted water into an irrigation ditch, "is my land. I installed that pump."

Not surprisingly the farmers of Qalqilya were bitter men. By the time I visited their village they had begun to infiltrate across the border at night, at first to steal fruit, then to commit sabotage, finally to kill Jews. To halt these depredations the Israeli army thrust across the frontier on the night of October 11, 1956, blew up Qalqilya's police station, and killed an estimated twenty-five Arabs. The raid, said Israeli spokesmen, was in reprisal against the "murder gangs" of Qalqilya.

I left Qalqilya convinced of two things—that the grievance of the town was real and that I must visit the Jewish village of Nir Eliahu in Israel, whose people now farmed the fields of Qalqilya, to hear their side of the story. This could not be done simply by passing through the line of white pillars, for those posts marked a hostile no-man's-land. I had to wait until my next journey to the Jewish state, in 1956.

To reach the Jewish settlement I drove along a dusty road through the Israeli coastal plain. At a fork in the road a sign confronted the traveler: STOP—FRONTIER AHEAD. The eastern fork led to Qalqilya, the western fork to Nir Eliahu. Two days before I arrived in the Jewish village, gunfire from Qalqilya had killed two policemen of the settlement and wounded a farmer. Thus,

Nazareth, once the capital of Galilee, is today the largest Arab city in the State of Israel. (Israel Government Tourist Office)

when I arrived, for every Jewish farmer tilling the fields another man of Nir Eliahu stood guard with a gun.

The buildings of Nir Eliahu still had a raw look, for the village was only a few years old. The average age of the settlers was twenty-one. The oldest man in the village, a tall, dark-haired Jew, was thirty-one. At noontime we all gathered in the communal dining hall, and the people of Nir Eliahu told me their tale.

During World War II a number of Jewish children, whose parents had been killed by the Nazis, were gathered together in Romania and sent to Palestine. There they were assigned to a *kibbutz,* or communal settlement, to learn how to farm. A similar group of Jewish orphans was collected in Turkey and also sent to Palestine. When the young people were eighteen years old, the two groups were brought together by the Israeli government and assigned to found a kibbutz of their own. The land they were given included the fields and orange groves of Qalqilya. The orphaned Jews named their new settlement Nir Eliahu and set to work, only to find themselves attacked by people they never had known—the Arabs of Qalqilya.

Who was right and who was wrong? The Arabs who had lost their lands and could not earn a living to support their families? Or the Jews whose parents had been killed in German concentration camps and who had been given a new home in Palestine? In this tangled story of two villages, there was no easy right or wrong. Innocent people on both sides had been caught up in a struggle larger than themselves, over which they had little or no control.

Years passed, bitterness grew. Then came the third round of Arab-Israeli fighting in June 1967, during which the Israeli army overran Qalqilya and all the kingdom of Jordan lying west of the Jordan River. Again I was in Israel and went to Nir Eliahu, now an established town, with trees lending shade to buildings which had been stark in the landscape eleven years before.

Where were the young Jews I had known? Scarcely a one remained in Nir Eliahu. Some had gone to help a new generation of pioneers to found *kibbutzim* elsewhere in Israel. Others had moved into cities and towns. Different people lived in Nir Eliahu and farmed the fields of Qalqilya. Did they still have trouble with Arabs across the way? A Jewish farmer shrugged. Oh yes, the raiders still came across—or they had, he added dryly, until a few days ago, when the Israeli army had seized the town.

I drove back along the road to the fork I remembered and turned toward Qalqilya. An Israeli soldier stopped me. I could not visit the town, despite the army pass I carried. Later I found out why. Qalqilya had been razed to the ground by Israeli tanks and explosives. Elsewhere in their conquest of the West Bank of Jordan in June 1967, the Israelis had left Arab towns largely untouched. But Qalqilya had been destroyed, apparently in reprisal for all the Jews killed by Qalqilyans over the years. Later the Arabs of Qalqilya were allowed to come back, and Israeli soldiers helped them rebuild their shattered town.

Today new actors walk the stage in Qalqilya and Nir Eliahu. People have been born, moved away, and died in both towns. But the problems and tension remain—rooted in mutual devotion to the same piece of land.

2

The Sons of Abraham

Few nations, of whatever size, command world attention as consistently as Israel. Almost since its inception in 1948, the modern State of Israel has been a source of tension between the United States and the Soviet Union. And no other problem has consumed as much debating time at the United Nations as the rivalry between two Semitic peoples, Arabs and Jews.

This rivalry can be summed up in one word—Palestine. Arabs and Jews each proclaim a fierce loyalty to the land where Abraham, father of the Jewish people, claimed to have received a covenant from God, and where Mohammed, Prophet of the Arabs, is said to have been miraculously transported by God from Arabia.

Of these two contending peoples, the Jews were the first to appear on the scene. Their recorded history, the story of Israel, began almost four thousand years ago, when a Semitic nomad named Abraham gathered up his family and flocks and set out from the land of the Twin Rivers westward toward the

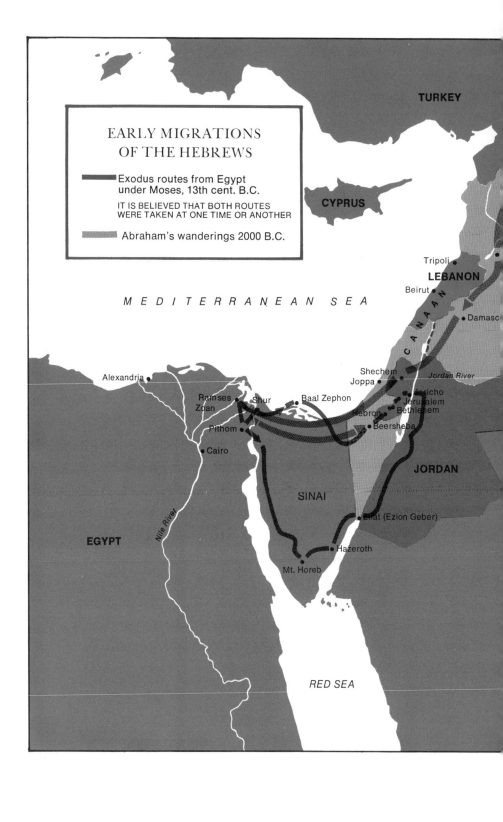

EARLY MIGRATIONS
OF THE HEBREWS

Exodus routes from Egypt
under Moses, 13th cent. B.C.

IT IS BELIEVED THAT BOTH ROUTES
WERE TAKEN AT ONE TIME OR ANOTHER

Abraham's wanderings 2000 B.C.

TURKEY

CYPRUS

Tripoli

LEBANON

Beirut

Damasc

MEDITERRANEAN SEA

CANAAN

Alexandria

Shechem
Joppa   Jordan River

Ramses   Shur   Baal Zephon   Jericho
Zoan   Jerusalem
                                    Hebron   Bethlehem
Pithom   Beersheba

Cairo

JORDAN

SINAI

Nile River

Eilat (Ezion Geber)

EGYPT

Hazeroth

Mt. Horeb

RED SEA

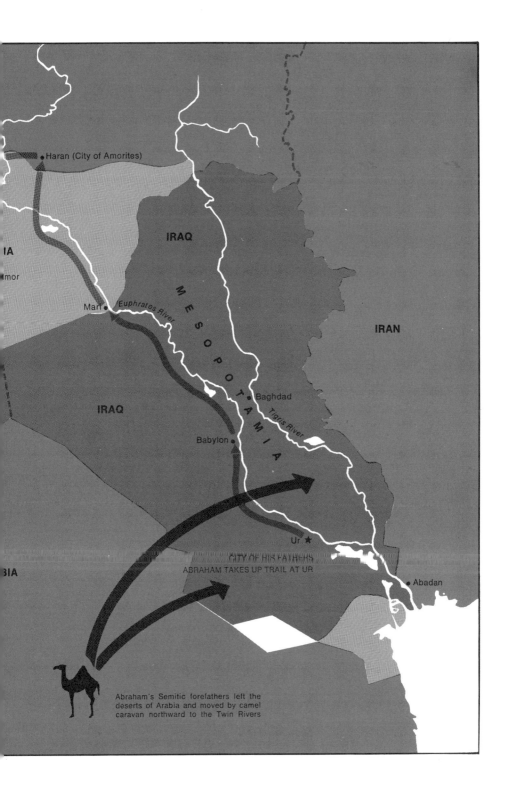

Haran (City of Amorites)

IA

mor

IRAQ

M
E
S
O
P
O
T
A
M
I
A

Mari • /Euphrates River

IRAN

Baghdad

IRAQ

Tigris River

Babylon •

Ur ★

CITY OF HIS FATHERS
ABRAHAM TAKES UP TRAIL AT UR

• Abadan

3IA

Abraham's Semitic forefathers left the
deserts of Arabia and moved by camel
caravan northward to the Twin Rivers

land of Canaan. The Tigris and Euphrates, the twin rivers whose banks Abraham abandoned, watered the plains of Mesopotamia, or modern Iraq, and made them green and fruitful for the mingled peoples—Babylonians, Chaldeans, and Assyrians—who farmed, traded, and built their cities by the great streams.

But within Abraham the Semite was an impulsion to move out from these settled lands toward a new horizon. In so doing, he was obeying the same restless urge which had impelled his own Semitic forefathers at some earlier time to leave the deserts of Arabia and move by camel caravan northward to the Twin Rivers. Now Abraham, about 2000 B.C., shook off the dust of Ur of the Chaldees, the city of his fathers, and took up the caravan trail.

At some point in his wanderings the patriarch became convinced that his steps were being directed by God toward a land of promise. "And I will give unto thee," the Scriptures describe God as saying to Abraham, "and to thy seed after thee, the

Nativity Square in Bethlehem. This ancient city is thought to date back to the time of Abraham. (Israel Government Tourist Office)

land wherein thou art a stranger, all the land of Canaan, for an everlasting possession" (Genesis 17:8). From this covenant, bequeathed to the "friend of God," as Abraham was called, stems the Jewish commitment to Palestine.

Abraham's tribe was known as the Hebrews, a name distinguishing his kin from other wandering peoples of the ancient Middle East. Finally, after years of sporadic movement, including a sojourn at the Amorite city of Haran, Abraham and his family pitched their black goat-hair tents in the central hill country of Canaan, or Palestine, the "promised land." Already Canaan was inhabited by a motley spread of peoples, all under general subservience to Egypt in the south. Indeed, during one prolonged drought in Canaan, the Hebrews themselves journeyed down for a stay in the fertile valley of the Nile.

In Palestine, two sons were born to Abraham—Isaac, son of Sarah, and Ishmael, son of Hagar, a bondwoman or slave. To Isaac passed the covenant of God, and later, when he was sightless and old, Isaac bestowed the mantle of leadership on his son Jacob.

Jacob became known as Israel, or "prince of God," and to this day the Hebrews, or Jews, are described as the children of Israel. Twelve sons were born to Israel, including Joseph, his favorite, to whom, the Bible tells us, Israel gave a coat of many colors. Inflamed by jealousy, Joseph's brothers sold him into slavery in Egypt, where Joseph, through his wisdom and his ability to divine dreams, rose to become the chief adviser to the pharaoh.

Famine struck again in Canaan, and the patriarch Israel, having learned that Joseph was alive, summoned his family and went down to Egypt to join his son. This happened about 1700 B.C. Decades passed, Israel and Joseph died, and a new dynasty of pharaohs arose who had not known Joseph. The Hebrews, no longer honored guests of the pharaohs, became their slaves. Toiling under the burning Egyptian sun to build the cities of Pithom and Ramses, the groaning Hebrew people accepted the leadership of Moses, to whom came a call from God to lead his people out of captivity in Egypt, back to Palestine.

For forty years Moses and his people wandered in the wilderness of Sinai. By the time they came to the heights of Moab, overlooking the Jordan River valley and the eastern part of Palestine, the Hebrews once again were a tough nomadic folk, perhaps six thousand strong.

To Joshua, Moses' successor, fell the task of conducting the battles that established the Hebrews once more in Palestine. Joshua's first conquest, about 1250 B.C., was the city of Jericho, lying in an oasis of palm trees in the midst of the arid Jordan valley. Then Joshua and his Hebrew warriors struck westward, defeating the Gibeonites and five Judean kings, until the land of Judah came under the Hebrew sway.

Moses brings his people safely across the Red Sea and makes the Pharaoh's legion drown. Painting in Saint-Germain-des-Prés, Paris. (The Bettmann Archive)

An oasis near the city of Jericho presents a green contrast to the wastes of the nearby Judean desert. (Israel Government Tourist Office)

Judah formed the mountainous heartland of southern Palestine. The central part of the country appears to have slipped without struggle under Jewish suzerainty. A campaign in Galilee added northern Palestine to the holdings of the twelve Hebrew tribes, named after the sons of Israel. This period of conquest ended about 1200 B.C., and for the next six hundred years the Hebrews were the dominant people of Palestine, reaching great prosperity under King David.

These centuries, however, were full of troubles. The twelve tribes were divided often among themselves, challenged by other Palestinian peoples, and threatened by conquest from outside powers. Persistent foes were the Philistines, whose giant champion, Goliath, the young David slew with a sling and a stone.

Through all these vicissitudes the sense of Jewish nationhood, based on Abraham's covenant with God, ripened into the conviction that the Hebrews were a "peculiar people," marked out by God and linked always to Palestine, the promised land. Jerusalem, one of the last Canaanite towns to fall to the He-

brews, became the spiritual and temporal capital of the Jews in
Palestine.

A unifying force among the twelve tribes was their common religion, codified by Moses during the years of wandering in
Sinai. Hebrew tradition held that, on a cloud-shrouded mount,
Moses had received the revelation of the Ten Commandments
and the Law. These teachings of Moses bound the Hebrews to
the worship of Jehovah and led them to the concept of a monotheistic God. Together, the Ten Commandments and the Law
regulated every detail—religious and temporal—of Hebrew life.

Then, in 721 B.C., disaster struck. The hosts of Sargon II,
king of Assyria, swept through northern Palestine and carried the
Hebrew people back to Mesopotamia, the same land of the Twin
Rivers which Abraham had left so many years before. The Diaspora, or dispersion of the Jews from Palestine, had begun. Two of
the twelve Hebrew tribes, centered on Jerusalem, held out until
586 B.C., when Nebuchadnezzar, king of Babylon and conqueror
of the Assyrians, captured Jerusalem and destroyed the Temple
of Solomon.

*A modern Israeli copper mine at the Negev site, near Eilat, where
King Solomon's copper mine is thought by some scholars to have
been located.*

Now the exile of Jews from Palestine was complete. Not until 1948, except for the interlude of the Maccabean Revolt, would the Jewish people again be sovereign in Palestine, the land they believed had been bequeathed to them by God. Through the long centuries of exile, scattered throughout Asia, Africa, Europe, and the Americas, the Jewish people remained constant to their dream, expressed in the prayer "Next year in Jerusalem." Next year, someday, the Jews would return to their promised land.

Destiny marked out the Arabs as the next great Semitic people in Palestine. We recall that Abraham, the Hebrew patriarch, had had two sons—Isaac, in whom the covenant was confirmed, and Ishmael, the child of an Egyptian slave woman named Hagar. Sarah, the mother of Isaac, was jealous of Hagar and persuaded Abraham to drive the bondwoman and her son into the wilderness.

God, according to the biblical story, visited Hagar in her distress and caused a well of water to spring out of the desert to save her child. He promised her that he would make of Ishmael "a great nation." The Lord said more about Ishmael—that "he will be a wild man; his hand will be against every man, and every man's hand against him" (Genesis 16:12).

Ishmael and his descendants, in other words, were to be nomads of the desert, wanderers dwelling in tents, avoiding the settled lands. The sons of Ishmael became known as Arabs—or, to put it another way, the Arabs trace their origin to Ishmael, elder son of Abraham. Thus Arabs and Jews, Semitic cousins, struggling so bitterly today over the promised land, hark back to Abraham as their common father.

While the ancient Hebrews were establishing themselves in Palestine, and later during the centuries of Jewish exile, the Arabs lived remotely, almost untouched by the outside world, in the harsh deserts of Arabia, a great peninsula lying southeast of Palestine. They lived in tribes, each with its own grazing grounds, and sometimes were allied to one another but more often at war. Then, in the seventh century after Christ, arose an Arab leader who gave a sense of common purpose to these disparate peoples of the desert. To a man named Mohammed, in the Arabian city of Mecca, came the vision of a new religion, which he called Islam, or submission to God. Like Judaism and Christianity, the two great Middle Eastern religions which had preceded Islam, Mohammed's new faith was monotheistic, that is, proclaimed the existence of only one universal God, named Allah.

Mohammed the Semite drew on the inspiration of earlier Semitic prophets. Jesus, John the Baptist, Elijah, Solomon, David, Moses, and, of course, Abraham—all these and other biblical figures loomed large in the teachings of Islam. The Koran, or holy book of Islam, bequeathed by Mohammed to his followers, denounced the worship of idols and images, just as Moses in his day had destroyed the golden calf idolized by the rebellious Hebrews in the wilderness of Sinai.

Five basic tasks, called the five pillars of Islam, were assigned to each Moslem, or follower of Mohammed. A Moslem acknowledged only one God, Allah, and Mohammed as his Prophet. Each day he repeated ritual prayers, which remain unchanged to the present. At certain seasons of the year Mohammed's people were required to fast. They gave alms to the poor. And, at least once in his lifetime, each Moslem was obliged to make a pilgrimage to Mecca, the holiest city of Islam, near the Red Sea coast of Arabia. Here, as part of his ritual, the pilgrim was to cast stones at the devil, at the place where Abraham was thought to have been tempted by Satan and to have escaped by throwing seven stones.

To die in battle for the Prophet not only made an appealing challenge to fierce nomads of the desert but held out the promise of Paradise. Swiftly Mohammed's religion spread throughout the Arabian Peninsula and then, zealously backed by

Bedouin shepherd. (Israel Government Tourist Office)

desert men accustomed to hardship and war, conquered the Middle East as a whole, including Palestine. One hundred years after Mohammed died in 632, his followers had created an Arab empire stretching from the borders of China through the Middle East, across North Africa, and into Spain.

Within this empire Palestine, holy land of the Jews, had special meaning to Moslems. Jerusalem, conquered by the Arabs in 638, was said to have known the presence of Mohammed himself, when Allah showed the holy city to the Prophet. Today, within the mellow stone walls of Old Jerusalem, the golden dome of the Mosque of Omar commemorates Mohammed's journey.

From the seventh century until 1948, when Arab and Jewish armies clashed in the Holy Land, Arabs were the dominant people of Palestine. They were not dominant in a political sense, for Christian Crusaders, Egyptian Mamelukes, Turks, and finally the British, after World War I, conquered and ruled Palestine in turn. But numerically Arabs formed the backbone of the land. To generations of Arabs living in the Holy Land—and, by extension, all Arabs—Palestine was home.

3

Zionism and the Exiled Jews

For more than two thousand years the Hebrews were not truly sovereign in Palestine. From 586 B.C., when Jerusalem fell to Nebuchadnezzar, until 1948, non-Jews ruled the promised land. Always, however, some Jews continued to live in Palestine, even though under alien control. Indeed, Cyrus the Great, whose Persian hosts had conquered Babylon, allowed a large group of Jews to trek westward and resettle in the Holy Land, following roughly the same route taken by Abraham at the dawn of Jewish history.

This colony reached a high point during the reign of the Persian king Artaxerxes I, who authorized two Hebrew leaders, Ezra the Scribe and Nehemiah, to reconstitute Jewish life in Palestine. Ezra reorganized Hebrew religious observance according to the teachings of Moses, embodied in the Pentateuch, or first five books of the Old Testament. Nehemiah was commissioned by Artaxerxes to rebuild the ruined walls of Jerusalem.

This work, completed in 444 B.C., ushered in the Second Jewish Commonwealth. Tolerant Persian kings allowed the Jews of Judea to develop and govern their internal affairs, paying taxes and political allegiance to the heirs of Cyrus the Great. The Persians, a non-Semitic race, ruled Palestine and the Mesopotamia area from their eastern kingdom in what today is called Iran.

Then Alexander of Macedon destroyed the Persian Empire and established Greek rule throughout the Middle East, including Palestine. When Alexander died at the age of thirty-three, the eastern part of his empire split in two. His successors, the Seleucids of Syria and the Ptolemies of Egypt, non-Semitic peoples who preceded the Arabs, struggled incessantly for control of the Middle East, using Palestine as a battlefield. The Jewish colony dwindled, with many Jews filtering north to Syria and others south to Egypt.

Under Judas Maccabeus (Judas the Hammerer), a Hebrew warrior who launched a revolt against the Seleucids, uneasy political control of Jerusalem and parts of Palestine was restored to

The rock fortress of Masada was the site of major drama in the first century when Jewish rebels put themselves to death rather than submit to the might of Rome. (Israel Government Tourist Office)

the Jews. Quarrels among the Maccabean descendants led to intervention by Pompey, the Roman general then in Syria, who seized Jerusalem for Rome in 63 B.C.

"Render therefore unto Caesar the things which are Caesar's; and unto God the things that are God's" (Matthew 22:21). These words by Jesus, responding to his enemies who had tried to trick him into expressing disloyalty to Rome, testified to Roman rule of Palestine at the time Christianity was founded.

The rule of the Caesars was followed by that of the Byzantine emperors of Constantinople, who ruled the eastern division of the later Roman Empire from 395 to 1453. The Byzantines, who founded the Eastern Orthodox Church, in turn yielded Palestine to the Arab followers of Mohammed the Prophet, who made the Holy Land into a Moslem province. The Arabs entered Palestine in the seventh century and, though they remained there as a people, the Arabs lost political control of the Holy Land to a succession of short-lived Middle Eastern dynasties.

From 1099, when Christian Crusaders from Europe captured Jerusalem, until 1291, the Holy Land was more or less under Christian domination. Saladin's Moslem Mamelukes, who expelled the Crusaders from the Middle East, were defeated by the Ottoman Turks, who had seized Constantinople in 1453 and pushed east, south, and west to found the Turkish Empire. Turkish control of Palestine lasted until the end of World War I, when the British took up their mandate over the Holy Land. The Turks, though they adopted Islam as their religion, were a non-Semitic people, unrelated to the Arabs. Modern Turkey, whose capital is Istanbul, remains Moslem, but is separate from the Arab world.

During these centuries of bewildering change in Palestine, the peoples of the Holy Land grew increasingly motley, with the earlier sharp distinctions separating such peoples as Hebrews, Philistines, and Phoenicians becoming blurred by cultural influences emanating from Rome, Greece, and Byzantium. By the time the Arabs became the numerically dominant people of the Holy Land, the Jews were a small minority.

With the arrival of the British in Palestine after World War I, our story approaches the present time and the foundation of the modern State of Israel. In the synagogues of the Diaspora, and in the hearts of countless Jews throughout the world, the dream of returning to Jerusalem, focal point of Jewish national life, had remained alive. But for centuries there was little the exiled Jews could do to make their dream come true. They lived not as a single community in one place, but were scattered throughout the continents. Often their overriding problem was to evade, or survive, persecution in the lands of their dispersion.

This peculiar people of the Lord, as the Bible called the Hebrews, endured second-class treatment, or worse, almost everywhere they lived. Hitler's Germany was not the first country to force Jews to wear a distinctive badge. The Fourth Lateran Council of the Roman Catholic Church, meeting in Rome in 1215, directed European Jews to wear a yellow patch on their clothing, to distinguish them from gentiles, or non-Jews. The same order was given by Henry II, king of Castile in the late fourteenth century, for the Jews of his realm.

Americans recall 1492 as the year when Christopher Columbus discovered the New World. That same year had a different meaning for the 300,000 Jews expelled from Spain by Ferdinand and Isabella, the monarchs who helped to launch Columbus on his way. Earlier, in 1096, Christian Crusaders, thirsting to rid the Holy Land of "infidel" Moslems, prefaced their work by killing more than 10,000 Jews in cities along the Rhine River in Germany.

Persecution of the exiled Jews was general throughout Europe in the Middle Ages. An exception was Holland, which, after the Protestant Reformation, gave refuge to Jews. The European pattern, in those places where Jews were not expelled altogether, required their confinement in ghettos, or separate areas of cities.

The Jewish quarter of Amsterdam. Engraving, 1880. (The Bettmann Archive)

Jews who ventured outside the ghettos into Christian parts of town often did so at their peril.

Many European rulers of the time forbade Jews to own land, to practice farming, or to become members of craft guilds. Jewish men, to support themselves, often were forced to become moneychangers, a trade associated in public thought with usury. Some of the great Jewish banking houses of modern Europe may owe their origins to this early exclusion of Jews from primary pursuits.

Western Europe, particularly after the French Revolution, gradually relaxed its strictures on Jews. By the late nineteenth century Jews were being given the rights of citizenship in France, Austria, Prussia, Italy, and other countries of western and central Europe.

Discrimination against Jews persisted in eastern Europe, particularly in czarist Russia, where periodic pogroms, or organized massacres, were conducted against Jewish communities. Apart from this overt terrorism, the czars progressively restricted

Russian Jews to a territory called the Pale of Settlement, in the Ukraine and other western parts of Russia. This Pale, though a large tract of land, was really an expanded form of the ghetto.

The Russian rulers further handicapped their Jewish subjects by causing Hebrew boys to be drafted for twenty-five years of army service. The purpose was to wean Jews away from their families, religion, and traditions.

In 1881 Russian royalists charged Jews with complicity in the assassination of Czar Alexander II. This allegation unleashed a new pogrom, in which Jewish communities were pillaged by angry Russian mobs. In 1887 the czarist government sought further to hobble Jewish advancement by restricting the number of Jewish boys allowed to attend high schools and universities. As a result of all this, Jews began to emigrate in large numbers from Russia, with an estimated 2 million going to the United States

Expulsion of Jews from St. Petersburg. Scene at the Baltic Railway Station. Drawing, 1891. (The Bettmann Archive)

alone between 1881 and 1914. This was a new dispersion, or rather, a moving of the Diaspora from the Old World to the New.

The situation of Jews in Poland had been somewhat better, partly because Polish nobles were forbidden by law to engage in commerce. Jews were even encouraged by the government to assume a commanding position in Polish commercial life. This advantage later turned against the Jews, when the developing Polish middle class was forced to compete with Jewish businessmen. Even more damaging were three partitions of Polish territory in the 1790s, which brought the bulk of Polish Jewry under Russian control.

Such was the general picture as the twentieth century dawned—legal equality for Jews in western Europe, continued discrimination against them in eastern Europe. Jews living in the two parts of Europe naturally developed sharply differing views of the world around them.

Western Jews on the whole gave primary consideration to their citizenship as Frenchmen, Germans, Britons, or whatever the case might be. Such Jews had "assimilated," by immersing themselves in the mainstream of gentile life. Some went so far as to convert from Judaism to Christianity.

To many Jews of eastern Europe, neither assimilation nor emigration provided an answer. These Jews, calling themselves Zionists, looked on their Jewish brethren and found them a rootless people, confined to mental and physical ghettos. Many ghetto Jews, cut off from normal contact with the outside world, had turned inward, to a warped preoccupation with the minutiae of Jewish life. The Diaspora, argued the Zionists, had had the effect of magnifying those qualities in the Jews which differentiated or separated them from the people among whom they lived. The natural result, as the Zionists saw it, was anti-Semitism, expressing itself subtly or virulently, depending on where the Jews lived and in what concentrations.

שפייז וועט געווינען דיא קריעג!

איהר קומט אהער צו געפינען פרייהייט.

יעצט מוזט איהר העלפען זיא צו בעשיצען.

מיר מוזען דיא עלליים פערזארגען מיט ווייץ.

לאזט קיין זאך ניט גיין אין נישעז

יוניטעד סטייטס שפייז פערוואלטונג.

A Hebrew-language poster showing immigrants arriving in the United States. (The Bettmann Archive)

To Zionists the only escape from perennial persecution lay in a return of the Jewish people to Palestine, the promised land. There the Jews would strike down roots into their own soil. They would become farmers, artisans, working in whatever medium they chose. The shackles of exile would drop away, and Jews would regard themselves as a "peculiar people" in the sense of having been chosen by God, but no longer as second class.

To build up a prosperous Jewish community in Palestine would not be enough. The Jews must have a political state of their own, as did Americans, Italians, Swiss, and all other peoples. Every exiled Jew would have the right to return to the Jewish state in Palestine. Only thus, the Zionists insisted, could a sense of national identity be restored to the scattered Jewish people.

This whole line of argument was rejected by assimilationist Jews. They claimed that, far from overcoming anti-Semitism, the Zionists through their activities would increase it. Gentiles would resent Jews demanding the privileges of citizenship in whatever lands they lived but expressing loyalty to an outside state.

Under these circumstances Zionism found its natural home and inspiration in Russia, where there was the least chance for Jews to assimilate. The name Zionism derived from Mount Zion, a hill in Jerusalem which had been a center of Hebrew life in ancient Palestine. King David's tomb is believed to be on this hill, whose very name—Zion—conjured up to all Jews, religious and nonreligious, the mingled glories and travails of their past.

In 1884 the Choveve Zion (Lovers of Zion) met in the Russian city of Pinsk to map plans for the Jewish return to Pales-

Mount Zion, adjacent to the walled section of Jerusalem. (Israel Government Tourist Office)

Theodor Herzl, Hungarian-born Austrian Jewish writer, was the founder of Zionism. (The Bettmann Archive)

tine. Working separately from the Choveve Zion was Theodor Herzl, an Austrian Jewish journalist, who in 1896 published a book called *The Jewish State.*

Herzl, the privileged western writer, and the leaders of Russia's oppressed Jewry had one thing in common—devotion to the promised land. In 1897 Herzl convened the First Zionist Congress in Basel, Switzerland. From then until his death in 1904 he headed the Zionist movement.

A World Zionist Organization was formed, whose "parliament," or debating forum, was the annual, later biennial, congress of Zionist representatives. Jews throughout the Diaspora were invited to contribute to a Zionist bank, called the Jewish Colonial Trust. In 1900 the Jewish National Fund was created, to purchase land in Palestine from Arab owners. This land would be leased to Jewish settlers, but title would be held permanently by the Fund in the name of the Jewish people.

Within this organizational framework, Zionist leaders worked to enlist diplomatic support for a Jewish return to Palestine. Britain was a focal point in this effort. In 1903 the British government offered the Jews an autonomous territory in Uganda, in British East Africa. Herzl, disclosing this offer to the Sixth Zionist Congress in Basel, stressed that the African territory should not be considered a permanent substitute for Palestine. But Uganda at least would give beleaguered eastern European Jews a place to escape from persecution.

At first the Zionist delegates expressed joy that a Great Power had made an offer of statehood to the Jews. On reflection, however, sentiment hardened quickly against Uganda. Russian Jews—the very ones who, in the western view, had stood to gain most from the African territory—took the lead in rejecting any solution for the Jewish people except a return to the promised land. Russian Zionists charged their western colleagues with having underestimated the age-old longing of the Jewish people for Palestine. Zionism, in the Russian view, existed only as a vehicle to reestablish the Jews in the Holy Land.

Formal rejection of the Uganda offer took place in 1905, at the Seventh Zionist Congress. Herzl had died, and the mantle of Zionist leadership was passing to the Russian wing of the movement, headed by Chaim Weizmann.

Dr. Weizmann became a British subject and served his new country as a chemist during World War I. This work, plus his Zionist activities, brought the former Russian Jew into contact with a number of British personalities, already sympathetic to the Zionist cause. Notable among them were Arthur James Balfour, who was later Britain's foreign secretary; Lloyd George, prime minister during the latter part of the war; and Winston Churchill, destined to be the great leader of Britain during World War II and later.

The concept urged on these and other prominent Britons by Weizmann was that the British government and Zionists

Chaim Weizmann, first president of Israel.

should cooperate in the Middle East. Weizmann foresaw a British mandate over Palestine after World War I. This would afford the Zionists a friendly climate to foster Jewish settlement and would, in addition, give the British a power base from which to help safeguard their Suez and overland lifelines to India.

The culmination of Dr. Weizmann's diplomatic efforts was the issuance by the British government, on November 2, 1917, of the Balfour Declaration, named after the foreign secretary. This famous document became the legal cornerstone of the future State of Israel:

> His Majesty's Government view with favor the establishment in Palestine of a National Home for the Jewish people, and will use their best endeavors to facilitate the achievement of this object, it being clearly understood that nothing shall be done which may prejudice the civil and religious rights of the existing non-Jewish communities in Palestine or the rights and political status enjoyed by Jews in any other country.

Three phrases stand out here. The words "National Home for the Jewish people" were understood by Zionists to be synonymous with a Jewish political state. The Arabs, as we shall see, disagreed.

Second, the clause describing the "civil and religious rights of the existing non-Jewish communities in Palestine" was designed by the British government to protect the indigenous Arabs of the Holy Land.

Finally, the phrase concerning "the rights and political status enjoyed by Jews in any other country" was meant to reassure assimilationists. Many British Jews, regarding themselves as loyal subjects of the British king, objected bitterly to the Zionist claim that Jewish loyalty properly should devolve on the future Zionist state.

The British government, during the course of World War I, made two other commitments, neither of which proved to be compatible with the Balfour Declaration. In 1916 Britain and France concluded the secret Sykes-Picot Agreement, under which the two powers agreed to divide the postwar Middle East. France was to exercise authority in Syria and Lebanon, while Britain was to control Palestine and Iraq.

Separately, the British government induced the Arabs to revolt against the Turks, who then occupied the Middle East, by promising the Arabs an independent kingdom of their own after the war. This kingdom, as the Arabs understood it, was to include Palestine. On the basis of this promise the Arabs, led by the Hashemite family of western Arabia, launched the Arab Revolt of 1916. The military campaigns which followed, culminating in the capture of Damascus, were celebrated through the writings of T. E. Lawrence (Lawrence of Arabia), one of the British officers who guided Arab forces in the field.

The British, then, had made conflicting promises to the Jews, to the Arabs, and to France. Knowledge of this confusion came to the Arabs when the new Communist government in Russia, having overthrown the czars, published the secret Sykes-Picot Agreement. To Sharif Hussein of Mecca and his sons, the

Hashemite rulers of western Arabia and protectors of the Moslem holy places, this agreement appeared to slice away part of the future Arab kingdom.

British officials replied that this was not the case, reminding Sharif Hussein that the description of the proposed Arab kingdom specifically had excluded the "districts of Mersin and Alexandretta, and portions of Syria lying to the west of the districts of Damascus, Homs, Hama, and Aleppo." These, generally, were Syrian and Lebanese areas, promised to the French under the Sykes-Picot Agreement.

The Arabs and British did not disagree on the definition of Palestine, which was taken by both sides to be the geographic entity lying south of Lebanon and Syria, including the Jordan River valley, and bounded on the west by the Sinai Peninsula and the Mediterranean Sea. The disagreement arose from Sharif Hussein's understanding that Palestine was to be part of the larger Arab kingdom, which also would embrace Lebanon, Syria, Iraq, and at least the western part of the vast Arabian Peninsula.

The Sharif's conception had come from the correspondence between himself and Sir Henry McMahon of Britain. This correspondence, laying the groundwork for the Arab Revolt against the Turks, had formulated Britain's promise of an independent Arab kingdom after the war.

The British, for their part, had foreseen the future Arab entity—apart from western Arabia, which the Hashemites already held—as being restricted largely to the territories which Britain itself hoped to dominate after the war; namely, Palestine and Iraq. At what point British suzerainty over these areas would yield to full Arab control was not specified. To the British government, Arab claims to their kingdom held second priority to the British need to hold a secure land bridge from the Mediterranean to India, jewel of the British Empire.

It must also be said, in British defense, that these conflicting agreements with the Jews, Arabs, and French had been negotiated during a world war whose outcome by no means had been certain. Britain's primary aim at the time of negotiating had been to enlist all possible forces against the Germans and, in the Middle East, their Turkish allies.

In this atmosphere the postwar peace conference convened in Paris, with Zionists and Arabs attending. A remarkable correspondence between an Arab prince and an American Jewish leader discloses that, even at this late point, cooperation between Arabs and Jews in Palestine appeared to be possible. In October 1918 Prince Feisal, third son of Sharif Hussein and commander of Arab forces during World War I, had entered Damascus at full gallop at the head of twelve hundred Bedouin tribesmen. By general consent Feisal was to be the future Arab king.

On March 3, 1919, Feisal addressed a letter to Felix Frankfurter, a member of the American Zionist delegation to the Paris peace conference and later an associate justice of the United States Supreme Court. The prince wrote:

> We feel that the Arabs and Jews are cousins in race, having suffered similar oppressions at the hands of powers stronger than themselves, and by a happy coincidence have been able to take the first step towards the attainment of their national ideals together.
>
> We Arabs, especially the educated among us, look with the deepest sympathy on the Zionist movement. Our deputation here in Paris is fully acquainted with the proposals submitted by the Zionist Organization to the Peace Conference, and we regard them as moderate and proper. We will do our best . . . to help them through: we will wish the Jews a most hearty welcome home.

Feisal went on to describe his close relations with Chaim Weizmann, culminating in a written agreement between the two men, forecasting Arab-Jewish cooperation in the Holy Land. "We are working together," declared Feisal in his letter to Frankfurter, "for a reformed and revived Near East, and our two movements complete one another."

The American Zionist leader replied warmly to the Arab prince, thanking him for his support of Zionism and expressing the view that "the Arabs and Jews are neighbors in territory; we cannot but live side by side as friends."

Here, surely, was a promising beginning. What went wrong that resulted in friction between these "cousins in race," leading to three Arab-Jewish wars since 1948? The fact is that Prince Feisal and Dr. Weizmann were talking about entirely different things. The Zionists were promising to respect Arab rights within a Palestine governed by Jews. Feisal was willing to welcome Jews "home" to an Arab-ruled Palestine, which would form part of his greater kingdom.

Feisal's view was based on the fact that the population of Palestine—and of the surrounding lands which he hoped to claim as his own—was predominantly Arab. Beyond this, the Arabs, though divided tribally and politically, shared an overall sense of community, springing from common history, language, and religion. This state of mind was called Pan-Arabism.

During this period President Woodrow Wilson sounded out Arab views by sending an American mission to the Middle East, headed by Dr. Henry C. King, president of Oberlin College, and Charles Crane, an industrialist. The report of the King-Crane commission opposed the creation of a Jewish state in Palestine. Instead, the commission recommended a unified Syria, including Syria, Lebanon, and Palestine.

The Arab peoples themselves, the commission emphasized, overwhelmingly favored an American mandate in the Middle East, if mandate there must be. Their second choice was British suzerainty. But in no case did the Arabs want the French to control them. At the end of World War I, in other words, the United States was the western power to whom the Arabs looked with the most hope and trust. Progressively, as we shall see, that reservoir of Arab goodwill was lost to Americans.

On April 20, 1920, mandates were assigned by the Allied Peace Conference, meeting at San Remo. France, as foreseen by the Sykes-Picot Agreement, secured Syria and Lebanon. To Britain fell control over Palestine and Iraq. The Palestine mandate required Britain to implement the Balfour Declaration, calling for a Jewish national home in the Holy Land. Excluded from this commitment was that portion of Palestine lying east of the Jordan River.

Meanwhile, a congress of Arab notables, meeting in Damascus in March 1920, proclaimed Feisal king of an independent Arab kingdom, which was to embrace Syria and Lebanon, the two areas mandated to France. In August of that year French forces deposed Feisal and forced the Hashemite leader to appeal to the British for protection. The latter installed Feisal as king of Iraq, Britain's newly mandated territory in the east.

Feisal's older brother, Amir Abdullah, gathered a Bedouin army in Arabia, with the aim of marching north to drive the French from Damascus and restore Feisal to his Syrian throne. To forestall a French-Arab clash, the British carved a territory from their Palestine and Iraq mandates, named it Transjordan ("across" the Jordan River), and gave this country to Abdullah to rule. Later Amir Abdullah elevated his title to king and called his realm the Hashemite Kingdom of Jordan.

Within Palestine itself the stage now was set for Arabs and Jews to meet head-on in a violent contest for the Holy Land.

4

Palestine Under Mandate

When Great Britain took up its Palestine mandate in 1920, there were 55,000 Jews living in the country. Many of these people had gone to the Holy Land from Russia during the First Aliya, or wave of immigration, dating from 1882 to 1904. These early settlers had depended for support, not on the World Zionist Organization, which was in its infancy, but on the philanthropy of Baron Edmond de Rothschild, a member of the great Jewish banking house of that name in Europe.

The tendency of Jewish settlers during the Rothschild era was to found small business enterprises, in which labor was provided by Arabs and management by Jews. This pattern changed during the Second Aliya, from 1904 to 1914, when many more Jews from Russia and other eastern European lands went to Palestine. The Second Aliya was sponsored by the World Zionist Organization and Zionist concepts of Jewish settlement on the land now came into force.

The Zionists, as we have seen, believed that only a return to Palestine could rescue the scattered and exiled Jews from the ghettos and reconstitute them as a nation. But some way had to be found to create an authentic Jewish environment in Palestine. Jews emigrating from Russia to other countries, including the United States, generally assimilated as best they could into the national patterns of their new homelands. This could not be the case in Palestine. Arabs living there were divided into two general classes—a land-owning elite and a peasant base. Neither of these groups offered an environment which the Jews wished to copy.

> How shall this nation [wrote Aaron David Gordon, an early Russian Zionist] throw off two thousand years of the Diaspora? We, an alienated people with no roots in the soil and who are thus deprived of the power of creativeness, a people who have lived as parasites in towns and to whom by force of circumstances this has become second nature, we must return to the soil, to independence, to nature, to a regenerated life of work.[1]

To Gordon the answer lay in creating a new type of social organization called a kibbutz, or collective settlement. The kibbutz, as Gordon and other Russian Zionists conceived it, would inculcate in Jewish pioneers a love of the land, basic agricultural skills, and subordination of the individual good to the needs of the nation—all essential qualities, if the Jews were to reestablish themselves on the harsh soil of Palestine.

To understand the modern State of Israel, we must grasp the concept of the kibbutz, even though, as we shall see, only 3 percent of modern Israelis live in kibbutzim. Imagine that you are a Jewish child, born and brought up in an Israeli communal village. You do not live with your parents, nor have you since babyhood. You eat, sleep, play, and have your schooling in the

[1] Joseph Baratz, A Village by the Jordan (New York: Roy Publishers, 1955), p. 83.

A kibbutz in the Negev desert. Three percent of modern Israelis live in communal settlements. (Israel Government Tourist Office)

children's quarter of the kibbutz. Each day, before the evening meal, you go to your parents' room in the adult section of the village, to spend an hour or more with them. This is virtually your only contact with your parents, unless you happen to see them during the course of their daily work.

Now turn the situation around and regard the system from the standpoint of the mother. She is not responsible for the daily care of her child, whose upbringing is entrusted to nurses and teachers chosen by the kibbutz membership. Instead, the Jewish mother in a kibbutz works on the land, or in the dairy, or cooks in the communal kitchen, or keeps the account books of the village. In short, the mother, like her husband, accepts the tasks allotted to her by the kibbutz council. Her sense of motherhood must be satisfied with the quiet hours of family life before the evening meal.

To many outsiders this might seem too great a sacrifice. Yet most parents and children do not complain about this aspect of kibbutz life. I have asked young *chaverim* (members of kibbutzim) if they did not feel a sense of emptiness, living apart from their parents. The idea seemed to strike them as novel.

"After all," they replied, "we see our mothers and fathers every day!"

Parents pointed out that the evening hours of family sharing generally took place in a relaxed atmosphere, free of friction. Mothers and fathers did not need to discipline their children, nor guide them, except by example. That was taken care of by chaverim especially trained for the work. The abrasions and small frustrations of daily living were said to be absent from the parent-child relationship of the kibbutz.

Some families leave the kibbutz system, to live in what outsiders would call a "normal" way. There is, in fact, a steady inflow and outflow of kibbutz populations. But the strains which cause individuals to leave the kibbutzim arise more often from the property aspect than from separation of parent and child.

All property in the kibbutz is communally owned. Members contribute their labor, and in turn their daily needs—groceries, bedding, toilet articles, furniture—are supplied from communal stocks owned by the kibbutz as a whole. In the beginning the concept of communal ownership was so heavily

Children in a kibbutz visiting with their parents in the adult section of the village before the evening meal.

Young members of a kibbutz working in a field. They are wearing the kova tembel, *a sailor hat worn inside-out and brim down. (Israel Government Tourist Office)*

emphasized that private ownership of even the smallest thing was frowned upon.

Gradually this severity was relaxed. Women grew tired of turning in their laundry and drawing fresh clothes which might or might not suit them. A husband and wife liked to brighten up the room they shared with personal mementos. They wanted a radio, or a small refrigerator for snacks, though they still took their meals in the communal dining hall.

The first kibbutzim were agricultural settlements, and most of them continue so today. But a number have become prosperous manufacturing towns, canning for export fruits and vegetables grown on the kibbutz farm or making light machinery and consumer goods of various kinds. One kibbutz turns out the most popular leather jackets in Israel. Another makes fashionable women's clothing. Still others operate guest houses for tourists, where outsiders can spend a weekend or vacation and gain an insight into communal sharing.

The basic principles of kibbutz life remain generally intact —communal ownership of property, separate living quarters for

Chairs are made in this kibbutz workshop.

parents and children, an exchange of the individual's labor for the supplying of his needs. The degree of variance from the norm differs from village to village. The single room shared by a man and wife has, in many kibbutzim, expanded into a small apartment, indistinguishable from a similar flat in an Israeli city or town. Some kibbutzim stretch out the time children spend with parents to several hours each day. A few allow the children to sleep in the parental flat.

In some kibbutzim members simply draw supplies from the communal stocks as they need them. In other villages the chaverim get "points" in return for their work. These points they may "spend" as they see fit, picking out what they want from kibbutz supplies. Or they may be compensated with money, which they use outside the community to buy things unavailable in the village.

The kibbutz will finance a member's education, at home or abroad, as far as his talent will take him. The *chaver*, the member of the kibbutz, is protected by the community from birth to death, in sickness and health. In return, he devotes his strength and intelligence to the settlement, which for its part is dedicated to the larger good of the Israeli state.

The early Russian Zionists developed the concept of the kibbutz from a number of sources, including the European scouting movement and German youth groups called Wandervögel. Aaron David Gordon stressed the religion of labor, a union that must take place between the Jewish pioneer, returning from exile, and the soil of the promised land.

Degania, the first kibbutz, was founded in 1909 near the Sea of Galilee. Gordon, though never a member of Degania, helped to shape the settlement's life, as an example for kibbutzim to come. One of the first children born in Degania was Moshe Dayan, who later became a famed general and defense minister of Israel. Today, according to the Israeli government, there are 235 kibbutzim in Israel, with populations ranging in each one from 60 to 2,000.

This means that 84,200 Israelis live in kibbutzim—only 3 percent of the population. But the kibbutz as an institution has been far more meaningful to Israel than these figures would imply. These communal villages, and the men and women who transformed marshes and stony fields into crop-bearing land, symbolized the Jewish return from exile to Palestine. Kibbutz activity gained a new impulse after the 1967 Arab-Jewish war, when young Jewish soldier-pioneers founded communal villages along Israel's tense frontiers with Jordan, Syria, and in the Sinai Peninsula.

"It is true," says an Israeli major, himself a chaver, "that only 3 percent of all Israelis live in kibbutzim. But in the army we find that up to 25 percent of noncommissioned officers come from kibbutzim. The percentage of kibbutz members," he added, "is even higher among paratroopers, commandos, and other special forces."

Several of Israel's cabinet ministers are chaverim. A large number of kibbutz members sit in the parliament. "The kibbutz system," summed up one Israeli, "still furnishes the elite of the nation." Other Israelis with whom I talked felt this was going too far. But even they admitted that the imprint of kibbutz life was stamped deeply on the image of Israel.

For those Israelis for whom kibbutz life was too demanding, the *moshav*—or cooperative village—was developed. Each family in a moshav owns its own house, land, and some farm equipment. But all families in the village pool their produce and sell it through a village cooperative, splitting the proceeds among them. The general assembly, or "town meeting," of the moshav elects a council, which approves new members and decides on the sale or transfer of farmland within the village. The moshav, unlike the kibbutz, allows each family to bring up its own children. Five percent of all Israelis live in 344 *moshavim,* and today the moshav, rather than the kibbutz, is the predominant form of agricultural settlement, though the pioneer elite of the land still centers in the kibbutz.

The moshav *shitufi* was developed, beginning in 1936, as a compromise between the kibbutz and the moshav. Like the kibbutz, the moshav shitufi is based on collective ownership of property. But each family, as in the moshav, lives in its own house and is responsible for cooking, laundry, and child care. The current number of moshavim *shitufiim* is 22, with populations in each one ranging from 60 to 300.

We turn now from this glimpse into the way Zionist pioneers settled themselves on the land to a consideration of the mandate period itself. In 1922 the British took a census in Palestine, which showed 752,000 persons living in the country. Of this total the Jewish community numbered 84,000, and the Arab population about 650,000. This census came during the Third Aliya, or wave of immigration, dating from 1919 to 1924. From then on Jewish immigration to Palestine swelled so rapidly that the tide was numbered in years, not Aliyas.

During the first ten years of the mandate, 99,806 Jewish immigrants flocked to Palestine, with nearly 34,000 newcomers arriving in 1925 alone. This rapid growth of the Jewish population, coupled with land-buying activities of the Zionists, quickened Arab alarm and hostility toward both the Jews and the British.

The Zionists, under British protection, utilized the mandate period to lay the foundations of the future Jewish state. Article 4 of the British mandate over Palestine had provided for the establishment of a Jewish Agency, to cooperate with the British in creating a national homeland for the Jews. A key function of this Agency was to screen prospective Jewish immigrants to Palestine. Armed with a certificate of eligibility from the Jewish Agency, the immigrant presented himself at a British consulate for a visa. He then traveled to Palestine, where he found a complex Jewish organization already at work.

The Jewish community had an elected Assembly, with limited rights of self-government granted by the British. This Assembly, made up of representatives of various political parties, selected a "cabinet," called the General Council, reflecting the political composition of the Assembly. On the economic side the General Federation of Labor, or Histadrut, marketed crops produced by kibbutzim and moshavim, founded industrial enterprises, ran schools and hospitals, and administered a social welfare system. Jewish education flourished, and in 1925 the Hebrew University was opened in Jerusalem.

Outside Palestine, meanwhile, the World Zionist Organization collected money to finance these activities. The president of the World Zionist Organization also headed the Jewish Agency. The Jewish National Fund continued to buy land in Palestine in the name of the Jewish people. In 1920 Jews had owned approximately 160,000 acres of land in Palestine. By 1929 an additional 128,000 acres had been acquired. More than 100

Jewish settlements were farming this land, while Jewish urban centers in Tel Aviv, Haifa, and Jerusalem were growing rapidly.

This whole structure resembled a state within a state, as indeed it was intended to be. The State of Israel which emerged in 1948 grew naturally from the institutions developed during the mandate period. Today, in modern Israel, Histadrut still plays a key role in the social and economic life of the country. The Israeli Knesset, or parliament, mirrors the political lineup of the old Assembly. And, to complete the transition, David Ben-Gurion, who headed the standing executive committee of the Jewish Agency in Palestine during the mandate, became the first prime minister of Israel. The first president was Chaim Weizmann, leader of the World Zionist Organization.

The Arab community, though numerically superior, was ill-equipped to compete with the tightly knit Jewish organization. Arab society in Palestine was not democratic, like the Jewish, but was split along traditional lines. A wealthy landowning oligarchy of Arab leaders stood apart from, and controlled the livelihood of, the mass of Arab peasantry.

In addition, Arab leadership felt betrayed by the British, who—as the Arabs saw it—were helping the Jews to create a political state in Palestine, in contradiction to the British pledge to Feisal. In 1922 the British government assured the Arabs that the purpose of the mandate was not to make Palestine "as Jewish as England is English," but to create a Jewish "community," based on religion and race. The British promised to hold Jewish immigration within the limits which Palestine could absorb without injuring Arab interests.

None of this, however, persuaded the Arabs to cooperate with mandate authorities. Arab leaders declined an offer by the British to create an Arab Agency, which would have had a voice in controlling Jewish immigration. Heading the Arab community in Palestine was Haj Amin el-Husseini, Grand Mufti, or Moslem religious leader, of Jerusalem. Allied with Haj Amin were Arab traditionalists, opposed to both the British and Jewish presences in Palestine. These conservatives dominated the Arab Executive, elected by the Palestine Arab Congress, and frustrated the efforts of liberal Arabs to introduce social reforms and grant more education to poor people of the cities and farms.

Some well-to-do Arab landowners did not hesitate to sell their land to Jewish settlers through the Jewish National Fund. This land not only was priced artificially high, but often consisted of malarial marshes, which Jewish pioneers had to drain and clear before kibbutzim could be founded.

In later years some Arab spokesmen charged that Jews bought the best land in Palestine. In fact, the Zionists paid exorbitant prices for tracts which Arab owners had often considered too poor to develop. It was not Arab peasants and tenant farmers, who have suffered greatly from the Arab-Jewish conflict, who sold land to the Jews. These sales came primarily from Arab aristocrats, who claimed to speak for the entire Arab community of Palestine.

Some Jews, too, dealt in land speculation in Palestine. These were what the Zionists called "capitalist" Jews, mostly from Poland, who had come to the Holy Land with a few thousand dollars each and little zeal for Zionism. Many of these non-Zionist Jews lost their savings during the economic depression which struck Palestine in the late 1920s, and emigrated to other lands.

Arab-Jewish riots led the British government to issue a White Paper in 1930, which declared that the economic situation in Palestine required the suspension of Jewish immigration and restrictions on land purchases by Jews. Jewish protests throughout the world, contending that the White Paper contravened Britain's obligation to the Jews under the mandate, caused the British government to reverse its policy.

Prime Minister Ramsay MacDonald, in a letter to Dr. Weizmann on February 13, 1931, affirmed that establishment of a Jewish national home remained a positive task of the British government. One result of the scrapping of the 1930 White Paper was a rising influx of Jewish immigrants, 182,839 of whom came to Palestine from 1930 to 1936. Twenty-seven percent of the newcomers in 1936 were German Jews, fleeing from Hitler's Third Reich.

Time and again in the mid-1930s the Arabs demanded an end to Jewish immigration and the halting of land sales to Jews. To reinforce their demands Arab political factions in Palestine combined their strength in the Arab Higher Committee in 1936. Mandate authorities, seeking to give the Arabs a larger role, in 1935 proposed a new Legislative Council for the country, weighted in favor of the Arabs. The British Parliament in London criticized the plan as inconsistent with Britain's mandate responsibilities toward the Jews and the project collapsed.

Arab frustration burst forth finally in prolonged violence, when Arab guerrillas killed Jews, destroyed their property, and bombed both Jewish and British installations in towns. Over three thousand persons were killed during the so-called Arab Rebellion from 1936 to 1939. Many of the casualties were Arab terrorists, shot by British troops.

The Jewish community now added the first elements of a military force to its political and economic structure. Orde Wingate, a young British officer, was assigned to train Jewish guerrilla forces, or Special Night Squads, to combat Arab terrorists. These squads formed the shock troops of the Jewish Haganah, an underground self-defense organization created to protect the kibbutzim.

In 1937 the British proposed the partition of Palestine into a Jewish state, an Arab state, and neutral enclaves around Jerusalem and Bethlehem. This plan foundered on the rock of Arab refusal to accept any sovereign Jewish entity in Palestine. Two years later the British tried another tack. A White Paper published in 1939 called for the creation in ten years of an independent Palestinian state, linked by special treaty to Britain. The country was to be divided into three zones. In one zone land transfers from Arabs to Jews were to be allowed, in a second they would be restricted, and in the third zone land transfers would be forbidden.

The Arabs complained that this scheme did not go far enough. The Zionists also opposed the plan, arguing that the British were abandoning their commitment to establish a national homeland for the Jews in Palestine. The Permanent Mandates Commission of the League of Nations agreed with the Zionist view.

Then came World War II, with its progressive revelation that Hitler's Third Reich was systematically exterminating European Jews. The pronounced goal of the Nazis was to erase the Jewish people from the earth. They failed. But 6 million Jews perished, many in the gas chambers of concentration camps scattered throughout Germany and occupied Europe. The Nazi pogrom reduced the world's Jewish population from 18 million to about 12 million and it has grown only slightly since that time.

The Nazi holocaust had several effects on the Palestine problem. First, Zionist leaders saw clearly that the salvation of the Jewish people depended on Allied victory in the war. The Jewish Agency called on all Jews to cooperate with Britain. Twenty-seven thousand Jews volunteered to serve with British military forces in Palestine. A Jewish Brigade Group formed in 1944 took part in the final stages of the Allied campaign in Italy. Palestine Arabs, too—12,000 of them—volunteered for British service.

Assimilationist and Zionist Jews outside Palestine forgot their differences in their common concern to rescue endangered Jews. World pressure mounted on the British to open the gates of the Holy Land to all Jews who could escape from Nazi Europe. But the British mandate authorities, charged with keeping order in Palestine, implemented the White Paper of 1939. They divided

Former prime minister David Ben-Gurion talks with an African leader.

the country into three land-transfer zones and restricted Jewish immigration. Thousands of Jews arriving by ship were turned away or interned on Cyprus and Mauritius. One leaky ship, the *Struma*, sank off the Turkish coast with its load of refugee Jews, after being refused permission to land in Palestine. Seven hundred and sixty-nine Jews were drowned.

The American Zionist Organization, meanwhile, convinced that Britain would adopt the 1939 White Paper as postwar policy, approved the so-called Biltmore Program, drawn up by David Ben-Gurion in Palestine. At the heart of this plan was a call for unlimited Jewish immigration to Palestine and the creation of a Jewish army. The Biltmore Program was adopted as official policy of the World Zionist Organization. The Zionists now had made clear their determination to restore all of Palestine to the Jews.

In the Holy Land itself, as World War II drew to a close, British-Zionist cooperation began to crumble. Two Jewish extremist groups, the Stern Gang and the Irgun Zvai Leumi, launched terrorist attacks on British installations, culminating in the assassination of Lord Moyne, British minister of state in the Middle East, in Cairo in 1944. These terrorist activities were denounced by world Zionist leaders.

Finally the British government, unable to achieve a solution in Palestine, and with British resources depleted by World War II, asked the United Nations to take over the tangled Arab-Jewish dispute. In May 1947 the General Assembly formed an eleven-nation United Nations Special Committee on Palestine (UNSCOP) and directed its members to go to the Holy Land and report their findings. The report proved to be a fateful document, whose reverberations still echo in gunfire in the Middle East.

UNSCOP recommended the creation as soon as possible of an independent and economically unified Palestine, with the UN

An Arabic sign at the entrance of a school in Bireh, outside Jerusalem, says, "Allah is the greatest, Palestine for the Arabs." (Arab Information Service)

The United Nations Special Committee on Palestine (UNSCOP) at its first meeting, May 26, 1947, at Lake Success, New York. (United Nations)

to assume an initial supervisory role. The report then broke down into majority and minority recommendations.

The majority plan, presented by seven nations, called for the establishment of a Jewish state, an Arab state, and an internationalized Jerusalem. The minority report, signed by three powers, recommended a federated Palestine, with Jewish and Arab cantons, or communities, exercising local autonomy over their internal affairs. Jewish immigration, in the minority view, should be allowed for three years, up to the ability of the Jewish canton to absorb newcomers.

Signing the majority plan were Canada, Czechoslovakia, Guatemala, the Netherlands, Peru, Sweden, and Uruguay. The minority report was presented by India, Iran, and Yugoslavia. Australia, the eleventh member of UNSCOP, subscribed to neither plan.

The Zionists endorsed the majority report, since this called for a separate Jewish state, though smaller than the Zionists would have liked. The Arabs preferred the minority plan, which provided for a unified Palestinian state, with no sovereign Jewish entity. On November 29, 1947, the United Nations voted to partition Palestine into separate Arab and Jewish states, as the majority of UNSCOP had recommended.

Thirty-three nations voted for partition, thirteen against, and ten abstained. Britain, as the mandatory power, did not vote. The United States and the Soviet Union, who later were to compete for influence in the Middle East, both approved partition.

Within Palestine, bands of Arab guerrillas attacked Jewish settlements. Jewish defense forces replied in kind. Britain, foreseeing no end to the mounting violence, ended its mandate over Palestine on May 14, 1948.

The same day the Zionists proclaimed the State of Israel. The first nation to recognize the new Jewish state was the United States, followed swiftly by the Soviet Union and by the United Nations itself. One day later the armies of five Arab nations— Egypt, Transjordan, Iraq, Syria, and Lebanon plus a token force from Saudi Arabia—invaded Palestine to block the establishment of a Jewish state.

5

Three Arab-Jewish Wars

On the surface it would appear that the Arabs should have won the Palestine war of 1948. Their regular armies totaled 170,000 men, backed up by 40 million people living in the five Arab countries involved. These armies invaded a Jewish state which had fewer than one million citizens and no army other than the self-defense organization Haganah.

But this impression of overwhelming Arab might was illusory. Consistently the Arabs neglected to unify their military commands, with the result that five Arab armies fought largely independently of each other. Added to this lack of coordination was ineptitude and corruption at home, resulting in faulty equipment for soldiers in the field. Saudi Arab Bedouins and Egyptian *fellahin* (peasants) from the Nile valley had little taste for war in Palestine, a country alien to them.

The Arab armies resembled an open hand with five fingers, each probing for weak spots. Haganah, by contrast, was a well-organized force with long experience of guerrilla warfare. Ha-

Land assigned to Israel by the UN partition plan of 1947 and the extra territory seized by the Israeli Army in 1948. Israel grew by more than 30 percent as a result of the first Arab-Jewish war.

ganah could strike back like a clenched fist at each of the separate Arab probes.

Equally important was the attitude of Zionist settlers. At the end of a centuries-long road of persecution, they knew the Jews had no place to go but Palestine. The Jews were imbued with a tough will to win. This was their war. To many of the invading Arab soldiers the war had scant meaning beyond a mystical call to Arab unity based on common religion and language.

The war opened on May 15, 1948, in an atmosphere of bitterness, engendered in part by the mass murder of the men, women, and children of the Palestine Arab village of Dair Yasin by the Irgun Zvai Leumi on April 9. The aim of this deliberate act of cruelty was to terrorize Arabs into abandoning their fields and homes and fleeing from Palestine.

Later in the war Jewish extremists assassinated Count Folke Bernadotte of Sweden, who had been named United Nations Mediator for Palestine by the Security Council. Bernadotte, whose job was to bring Arab-Jewish fighting to a halt, had recommended to the General Assembly a change in the UN partition plan which would have given the Negev to the Arabs. Israel would receive in exchange part of western Galilee, which had been assigned to the Arabs under the partition plan. The exchange proposed by the Mediator would have given Egypt a land link to the eastern Arab states.

This recommendation cost Count Bernadotte his life. Jewish extremists were determined that no inch of territory assigned to the Zionist state under the partition plan should be awarded to the Arabs.

A majority of Jews inside and outside Palestine condemned the Dair Yasin massacre and the assassination by the Stern Gang of Bernadotte. Yet many Jews, while criticizing the methods employed by extremists, welcomed the flight of Arabs from the Holy Land. This made easier the establishment of a Jewish state. Gradually Jewish terrorist forces were absorbed within the larger

Count Folke Bernadotte, United Nations Mediator for Palestine. He was assassinated by Jewish extremists. (United Nations)

Jewish community, and today Menahem Begin, founder of the Irgun Zvai Leumi, sits as a deputy in the Israeli Knesset.

The war, broken by two brief truces, ended on January 7, 1949, in a clear victory for the Jews. Arab armies, with the exception of the British-trained Arab Legion of Transjordan, had been decisively defeated. This Jewish victory had profound implications for the future of the Middle East.

First, Israel had added 2,380 square miles, mostly in the Negev and western Galilee, to the 5,670 square miles which had been assigned to it by the UN partition plan. Israel ended up 30 percent larger than UNSCOP had recommended.

Second, approximately 700,000 Palestine Arabs had fled to surrounding Arab countries, creating a refugee problem which still has not been solved. In part these Arabs, with the memory of Dair Yasin fresh in their minds, fled because of their fear of what the Jews might do to them. Other refugees left at the urging of their own Arab leaders, who wanted the battlefield cleared of civilians.

Third, King Abdullah of Transjordan unilaterally annexed to Transjordan all of Palestine not occupied by the Jews. This gave Jordan a thick bulge of land west of the Jordan River, almost cutting the infant Jewish state in two. King Abdullah renamed his country the Hashemite Kingdom of Jordan and gave Jordanian citizenship to the 400,000 Palestine Arabs who sought refuge in his realm.

Finally, the Arab peoples were shocked and humiliated by their defeat and they strengthened their resolve one day to avenge themselves against the Jews. Gone now was any pretense of the Arab-Jewish cooperation that had been forecast by Prince Feisal and Chaim Weizmann. The Arab states refused to make peace with Israel. The most they would do was to sign armistice agreements, pending a final settlement of boundary and other disputes.

That settlement never came. The armistice lines froze into permanence. Because they had been designed to be temporary, the lines were drawn on the basis of battlefield gains. This gave rise to inequities, typified by the artificial division of Qalqilya between Israel and Jordan.

In the years that followed, the United Nations developed complex machinery to supervise the uneasy truce. A United Nations Truce Supervision Organization (UNTSO) was formed, to act as a buffer along the sensitive frontiers. This organization assigned separate teams of military observers, or Mixed Armistice Commissions, to mediate frontier disputes and forward their findings to the UN in New York. Each commission included Arab and Israeli officers, with a neutral chairman.

On the civilian side, the United Nations Relief and Works Agency for Palestine Refugees in the Near East (UNRWA) was created to administer to Arab refugees made homeless by the 1948 war. Each year member states of the United Nations vote funds to give basic food and clothing to these hapless people, plus some money to teach young refugees skills that might enable them to break out of camp life and become productive members of Arab society.

Qalqilya was only one among many places along Israel's tense frontiers where Arab terrorists slipped across armistice lines to commit sabotage and kill Jews. Beginning in 1953 Israel decided on a policy of massive reprisal to combat these depredations. During an October night in 1953 a battalion of the Israeli army swept across the Jordanian border and killed more than fifty Arab men, women, and children in the village of Qibya. For this raid Israel was condemned by the United Nations. Israeli spokesmen retorted that fewer Arabs had been killed in this punitive raid than the number of Jews murdered over a period of time by infiltrators operating from Jordan.

By this time the ruler of Jordan was young King Hussein, grandson of Abdullah. On July 20, 1951, King Abdullah had been killed by an Arab assassin as he entered Jerusalem's al-Aqsa mosque to pray. The king's "crime," in the eyes of many Arabs, had been to conduct secret talks with Israeli officials, in the hope of reaching a settlement that would give Jordan access to the Mediterranean Sea.

The Qibya raid failed to deter Arab marauders, and the Israeli army repeated its retaliation raids, against the Jordanian village of Nahhalin in 1954 and, as we have seen, against Qalqilya in 1956. To the north, meanwhile, Syrian gun positions on the Golan Heights persistently sniped down on Israeli fishing boats hauling their nets in the Sea of Galilee. In December 1955 the Israeli army launched a reprisal raid against these gun positions, killing forty-nine Syrians. Once more Israel was condemned by the Security Council.

Council members understood and in some cases sympathized with the reasoning that promoted the Israeli retaliations. But the council argued that Israel's duty was to work for redress through the peacekeeping machinery established by the United Nations along Arab-Jewish frontiers.

On one occasion, when two Israeli farmers were slain near the Syrian border, Israel did appeal to the Security Council instead of conducting a raid. The United States and Britain introduced a resolution condemning the "wanton murder" of the two Israelis. This resolution was vetoed by the Soviet Union, which by this time had swung its support to the Arab side.

In Egypt, meanwhile, an army junta led by Lt. Col. Gamal Abdel Nasser had overthrown King Farouk in July 1952. Nasser exiled the king and established an Egyptian republic, whose prime minister and, later, president he became. At first Nasser, preoccupied by Egypt's overpopulation and poverty, appeared to assign secondary importance to the Palestine problem. He did, however, allow Arab guerrillas to use the Gaza Strip, occupied by the Egyptian army during the 1948 war, as a base for raids into Israel. Arab infiltrators from Gaza began to mine Israeli roads and blow up water pipelines and bridges. This campaign was systematic in nature, as opposed to the unorganized activities of marauders from Jordan.

In February 1955 the Israeli army struck back at the Egyptian army in Gaza, killing thirty-eight Egyptian soldiers. The Egyptian response was to organize squads of Arab *fedayeen*, or commandos, and send them into the Jewish state to create terror. These fedayeen squads, operating under the command of an Egyptian army colonel, later extended their activities to Syria and Jordan.

Nasser later claimed that the Israeli raid of February 1955 finally convinced him of Israel's aggressive intentions and propelled him into a search for foreign weapons. This search, as we shall see, allowed the Soviet Union to penetrate the Middle East, where today it plays a major role. The Israelis, for their part, saw in Colonel Nasser their principal enemy.

By the fall of 1956 tension along Arab-Israel frontiers was

An Israeli officer uses a diagram in sand as he briefs his troops on action in the Sinai Peninsula, October 31, 1956. (Wide World Photos)

at the breaking point. On October 29, 1956, a force of 32,000 Israeli soldiers stormed into the Sinai Peninsula with orders to destroy the nests of fedayeen and clear out the Egyptian army. In seven days of desert warfare Israeli tank and motorized columns thrust through Sinai and reached the Suez Canal. The second Arab-Jewish war, like the first in 1948, ended in a debacle for the Arabs—in this case the Egyptians.

But Israel was not the only aggressor in 1956. By air and sea French and British military forces also attacked Egypt, whose President Nasser had abruptly nationalized the Suez Canal, the vital waterway linking Europe to Asia. Led by the United States and the Soviet Union, the United Nations demanded a ceasefire and the evacuation of invading troops from Egypt. Britain and France, unable to resist intense pressure from the United States, withdrew their last troops from Egypt in December 1956.

Israel was more slow to comply. Only when President Dwight D. Eisenhower threatened to invoke economic sanctions against the Jewish state did Israel order its army to withdraw from Sinai. This retreat was completed in March 1957.

Israel had lost the fruits of its military victory. Yet it did gain one advantage. The UN expanded its peacekeeping apparatus in the Middle East by forming a United Nations Emergency Force (UNEF), staffed by soldiers from neutral countries. These blue-helmeted troops took up positions along the Gaza Strip and at the southern tip of the Sinai Peninsula, at a place called Sharm el-Sheikh. The protective presence of UNEF opened the Red Sea passage to Israeli shipping, operating from the southern port of Eilat. No longer did the barrels of Egyptian guns, emplaced at Sharm el-Sheikh and on the tiny islands of Tiran and Sanafir, threaten Israeli vessels in the Strait of Tiran.

Israel's desert port of Eilat began to thrive. Oil from Iran could be shipped to Eilat and then pumped by pipeline up through the Negev wilderness to the towns and cities of the Jewish state. Israeli exports to East Africa and Asia no longer had to make the long haul across the Mediterranean Sea and around Africa. The Israeli government warned that the removal of UNEF troops from Sharm el-Sheikh would constitute an act of war.

Until the Sinai campaign of 1956, Israeli shipping had been barred from the Suez Canal by Egypt, as part of the general Arab economic boycott of the Jewish state. Following the 1956 war, when the canal had been cleared of sunken ships, Egypt for a time allowed Israeli cargoes to transit the waterway. Arrangements to this end had been negotiated by UN secretary-general Dag Hammarskjold, backed by pressure on Cairo from major western powers, including the United States.

Western governments stressed to President Nasser that his blockade of the Suez Canal to Israeli shipping appeared to flout three international undertakings. The Constantinople Convention of 1888 had guaranteed freedom of passage through the

UN secretary-general Dag Hammarskjold (left) and Egyptian president Gamal Abdel Nasser during talks in Cairo in November 1956. (United Nations)

Suez Canal. A Security Council resolution of September 1, 1951, had urged Egypt to stop interfering with the canal. Finally, President Nasser himself had declared in April 1957 that he would respect the terms of the Constantinople Convention.

On the basis of this promise Nasser allowed some forty Israeli cargoes to pass through the canal. Then, in March 1959, Egypt again closed the waterway to the Jewish state. To justify its action Egypt cited Article 10 of the Constantinople Convention, which provided that freedom of passage "shall not interfere with measures Egypt might find necessary to take to secure the defense of Egypt."

In vain Hammarskjold sought to reverse the Egyptian position through a compromise agreement. In December 1959 the Egyptians halted the Greek ship *Astypalea,* southbound for Djibouti with a cargo of Israeli cement. Eventually the *Astypalea* was forced to unload its freight at Port Said and sail away empty.

Since then no Israeli cargoes are known to have passed through the Suez Canal.

The following years were marked by the swift growth of Soviet influence in the Arab world. Seizing on Arab hatred of Israel as a pretext, the Soviet Union gained Arab favor by selling vast quantities of sophisticated weaponry first to Egypt, then to Syria and Iraq. Cairo in particular deepened its dependence on the Soviet Union, by mortgaging Egyptian cotton crops into the future to pay for these arms.

The influx of Soviet weapons posed a new problem for Israel. The primary threat, as Israeli generals saw it, was a buildup of Egyptian land and air forces on the Sinai Peninsula. By the spring of 1967 most of the Egyptian army was based at Sinai. Egyptian airfields also dotted the peninsula, as well as batteries of Soviet SAM-2 (surface-to-air) missiles, designed to destroy incoming enemy aircraft.

Whether President Nasser planned to use his army's new might to launch an attack on Israel is disputed. Nasser later denied that he had so intended. But he did point a finger of warning at growing clashes between Israeli and Syrian forces in the Golan Heights area. Should Israel attack Syria, Nasser asserted, Egyptian forces would retaliate by assaulting the Jewish state from Sinai.

Then the Egyptian president made a fateful move. He ordered UNEF out of Sinai and Sharm el-Sheikh, both of which were Egyptian territory, and closed the Strait of Tiran to Israeli shipping. The Zionist state now was back where it had been in 1956, when Israeli trade had no water outlet except the Mediterranean Sea. In one respect the 1967 situation was worse, for Israel now was confronted by a far stronger Egyptian army than before.

The Israeli government, as it had warned it would, regarded the removal of UNEF as an act of war. The question was, How should Israel react? If Israeli forces sat tight, waiting for

Arab armies to make the first aggressive move, Jewish cities might be devastated by Egyptian bombers. The alternative was for Israel to launch a preventive attack, hoping to catch Egyptian forces by surprise and to destroy President Nasser's Soviet-built air force on the ground.

Israel chose the latter tactic. On the morning of June 5, 1967, French-built jets of the Israeli air force streaked low across the Mediterranean Sea and over Sinai and blasted the Egyptian air force into ruins. Egypt's jet fighters and bombers, purchased by the labor of Egyptian fellahin raising cotton in the Nile valley, were destroyed on the ground by Israeli rocket-firing pilots.

At the same time tanks and trucks of the Israeli army rumbled across the frontier into Gaza and Sinai. On the sixth day of the war Israeli troops had crossed the sandy wastes of the Sinai Peninsula and had reached the east bank of the Suez Canal, routing the Egyptian army.

Part of the Yugoslav contingent of the United Nations Emergency Force (UNEF) on duty in the Sinai Peninsula after Israeli units had begun their withdrawal in December 1956. (United Nations)

Meanwhile, the Israeli government had sent a message to King Hussein of Jordan, through Lieutenant General Odd Bull, Norwegian commander of UN peacekeeping forces in Palestine. Israel, the king was told, did not intend to attack Jordan. King Hussein should keep his army out of the war. At the same time, however, the young Jordanian monarch received a message from President Nasser. The Egyptian leader, speaking to Hussein by telephone from Cairo, painted a picture of Egyptian warplanes in the skies over Israel, even though, at that moment, his air force lay smoking on the ground. Jordan should attack the Jewish state from the east, Nasser urged, and together Arab forces would press on to victory.

Hussein, in what proved to be the most costly mistake of his career, chose to heed Nasser and not Israel. The king ordered the Jordanian air force and artillery into action. Jordanian troops fought bravely, so much so that Israeli tank commanders saluted the courage of their fallen Arab foes. But the Jordanian army and air force, no match for the Israelis, were decimated, as Egypt's had been in Sinai. Jordan lost the Old City of Jerusalem and all the West Bank—that part of Palestine which had been annexed to Jordan in 1949 by Hussein's grandfather, King Abdullah.

With the eastern and southern fronts subdued, Israeli forces moved north against Syrian positions on the Golan Heights. By nightfall of June 10 Israeli troops had stormed the hills and driven out the Syrian army, and the six-day blitzkrieg was over. Israel had won the third Arab-Israel war as conclusively as the first two.

The outcome of the June war redrew the map of the Middle East. Only Israel's border with Lebanon, which had stayed out of the fighting, remained unchanged. Syria lost the Golan Heights to the Zionist state. The fighting left Jordan economically unviable, for that portion of the kingdom lying west of the Jordan River, now occupied by Israel, was the richest part of King Hussein's realm. Four-fifths of what the king had left was

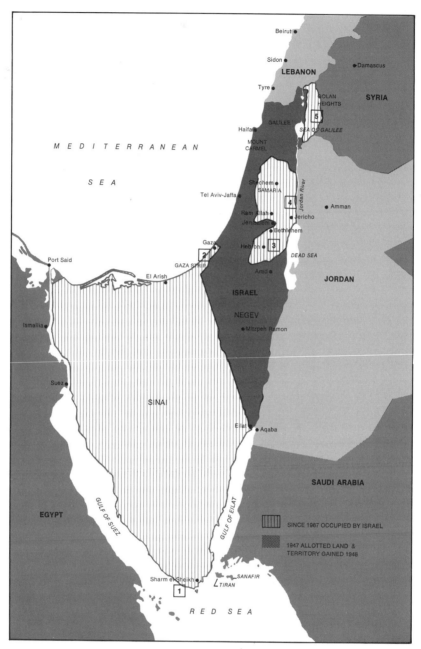

The five conquests of the 1967 war that Israel insists upon retaining in any ultimate peace settlement are: (1) Sharm el-Sheikh, which controls access to the port of Eilat; (2) the Gaza Strip; (3) East Jerusalem; (4) control of the Jordan River frontier; (5) the Golan Heights, which dominate northern Israeli settlements.

Two Arabs stand in front of the Jebel Hussein Camp, near Amman, Jordan. The camp is one of many set up by the United Nations Relief and Works Agency (UNRWA) for Palestine refugees in the Near East. (United Nations)

desert, crowded with refugees from Palestine. Egypt was driven from the Gaza Strip and all of Sinai, including Sharm el-Sheikh.

Before the 1967 war Arab governments had demanded that Israel take back those Palestine Arab refugees who had lost their homes in 1948. Refugees who did not wish to return to what now was a Jewish country should receive compensation for their lands and property, in the Arab view. A UN resolution supported this view.

Now, following the 1967 fighting, Egypt, Jordan, and Syria had a new requirement. They wanted to get back their *own* lands, lost for the first time to the Jews. A resolution passed by the Security Council on November 22, 1967, called on Israel to withdraw its "armed forces from territories occupied in the recent conflict." The resolution went on to demand "respect for and acknowledgement of the sovereignty, territorial integrity and political independence of every State" in the Middle East. Each country, furthermore, should have the right to live in peace "within secure and recognized boundaries free from threats or acts of force."

The Arabs insisted that Israel must withdraw from occupied territories before a discussion of these other points could follow. Israel demanded a clear definition of "secure and recognized" boundaries before calling back its troops. The result was that the "temporary" armistice lines of 1948 were replaced by the even more fragile ceasefire lines of 1967.

Nor is this the end of the problem, from Israel's point of view. At the beginning of 1968, six months after the June war, the Zionist state counted 2,773,900 citizens. Of this total 2,-383,900 were Jews and approximately 390,000 were Arabs. The latter included those Palestine Arabs who had remained in Israel after the first Arab-Jewish war, plus 70,000 Arabs of the Old City of Jerusalem, to whom Israel gave the status of "permanent residents" after the 1967 hostilities.

The loyalty to Israel of many of its Arab citizens is doubtful. These people did not choose to live in the Zionist state, but were trapped there, so to speak, after successive rounds of Arab-Jewish fighting. The Six Day War brought another 995,000 Arabs under Israeli control, including 599,000 living on the West Bank. Another 356,000 Arabs inhabited the Gaza Strip, also captured by Israeli troops in 1967. Thirty-three thousand Arabs occupied oases in the northern Sinai Peninsula, and 6,400 Syrians lived on the Israeli-occupied Golan Heights.

Willy-nilly, Israel is responsible for the welfare of these nearly one million Arabs until a peace settlement is achieved. The Israeli army has the capacity to rule Arab territories indefinitely as an occupation force. But most Israelis reject the concept of their nation as a colonial power. The alternative is for Israel to give citizenship to those Arabs under its control, as it did to Arabs left in Palestine after 1948 and, in a partial sense, to the people of Old Jerusalem in 1967. But Israel could not absorb an additional one million Arabs without losing its character as a

Jewish nation. The Zionist dream, "next year in Jerusalem," was predicated on the establishment of a Jewish national homeland in Palestine, not on the foundation of a binational Arab-Jewish state.

Three times Arabs and Jews have tested their antagonisms on the field of battle. Each time the Israelis have won, scoring fresh wounds in Arab pride and strengthening Arab resolve not to bow to an imposed peace.

6

Israel and the Arabs

Israel's attitude toward the Arabs differs country by country, conditioned by how each Arab government regards the Zionist state. The various Arab outlooks, in turn, stem from the complex history which divided the Arab world into many separate entities.

Arab warriors, we recall, burst out of the deserts of Arabia in the seventh century and created an empire covering the entire Middle East, North Africa, Spain, and even parts of southern France. This empire, with its capital first in Damascus, then in Baghdad, gradually splintered into various fiefdoms and minor dynasties, often warring with each other, but bound together by the mystical concept of pan-Arabism—common allegiance to the Arabic language and to Islam.

Fragmentation of the Arab empire was hastened by the conquest of the Middle East and North Africa by the Turks, who organized the Arab world in administrative districts, called *vilayets*.

The Turks in turn gave way to colonizing efforts by France and Britain, who not only divided the Arab world between them but assigned political frontiers to the Arab states. These frontiers have continued more or less intact to the present.

Israel is primarily concerned with those Arab countries which border the Jewish state. Directly north of Israel lies Lebanon, a country of 2,600,000 people—smaller in size and population than Israel. Lebanon's population is divided roughly half and half between Christian Arabs and Moslem Arabs, a situation unique in the Arab world. At times Moslem-Christian rivalry has broken out into civil war in Lebanon.

Potential frictions within the Lebanese community impel the Lebanese government in Beirut to avoid, so far as possible, foreign entanglements. Lebanon pays lip service to the general Arab hostility to Israel and has been forced by Moslem public opinion to allow Arab commandos to operate against Israel from bases in Lebanon.

These fedayeen activities have drawn reprisal raids from Israel into south Lebanon. On a wider scale, however, Lebanon poses no threat to Israel, and many Lebanese—a people famed as traders—would welcome peace with Israel, which forms a natural export market for Lebanese goods.

East of Lebanon and also abutting on Israel is Syria, a nation which consistently has been hostile to the Zionist state. Although Syria signed an armistice agreement with Israel in 1949, a succession of weak Syrian governments in Damascus has used the Palestine issue to whip up popular support among the roughly six million Syrians, most of whom are Moslem.

In February 1958 Syria joined with Egypt in the United Arab Republic, under the overall leadership of President Nasser. The union was awkward, not only because the two countries were geographically separated by Israel but because the Syrians of the plains and the Egyptians of the Nile valley had very different histories and interests. In 1961 Syria withdrew from the union, but President Nasser continued to refer to Egypt as the United Arab Republic (UAR).

The point of greatest friction between Israel and Syria was the Golan Heights, from which, as we have seen, Syrian guns fired on Israeli fishing boats on the Sea of Galilee. Israel seized the heights in 1967 and Syria today presents little military threat to the Zionist state.

South of Syria and sharing a long frontier with Israel is Jordan, the state carved out of the desert by the British after World War I to placate Amir Abdullah. This barren little kingdom was helped financially first by Britain, then by the United States. The complex relations between Jordan and Israel, centering on the West Bank and Jerusalem, are described later in the chapter.

East of Jordan and possessing no common frontier with Israel lies Iraq, known in ancient times as Mesopotamia, from which Abraham began his long trek to the promised land. Prince Feisal, having been chased from his Damascus throne by the French after World War I, became king of Iraq. The throne passed eventually to his grandson, also named Feisal, who was a cousin of King Hussein of Jordan. In 1958 King Feisal was assassinated by Iraqi army officers and the country thereafter became a republic.

Consistently Iraq's government and nine million people have expressed enmity to Israel. Alone among the nations that fought against the establishment of a Jewish state in 1948, Iraq refused to sign an armistice. In 1969 Iraq aroused Israeli anger by hanging nine Iraqi Jews as Israeli spies. Despite its hostility, Iraq is too weak militarily, and too far away geographically, to threaten Israel.

The vast Arabian desert which gave birth to Islam now is known as the Kingdom of Saudi Arabia, ruled by King Feisal, no relation to the Feisals mentioned above. In 1902 a tribal leader named Abdul Aziz ibn Saud began a career of conquest which, by 1926, embraced nine-tenths of the Arabian Peninsula, twelve times the size of New England. The Hejaz in western Arabia became part of Saudi Arabia, when Ibn Saud, called by his tribal followers the "Lion of the Desert," wrested it from Sharif Hussein, the man who had negotiated the Arab Revolt with Britain.

Today the sons of Ibn Saud govern a land which has become rich through the discovery of oil by American companies. King Feisal, head of one of the most conservative dynasties on earth, echoes Arab hostility to Israel. But in fact most of the eight million people of Saudi Arabia, scattered thinly across the oases and hot deserts of Arabia, have little direct involvement with the Palestine problem.

Along the fringes of the Arabian Peninsula, between Saudi Arabia and the sea, runs a string of minor sheikdoms. Some of these, like Kuwait and Qatar, are rich through oil. Others are poor. These sheikdoms, plus Yemen and South Yemen at the southern tip of the peninsula, play little role in the Arab-Israel dispute.

By far the most important Arab country is the United Arab Republic, or Egypt, Israel's neighbor to the west. President Nasser aspired to leadership of the Arab world. His successor, President Anwar el-Sadat, so far has confined himself largely to Egyptian affairs. Egypt's problems are enormous. Although the country is almost as large as Texas and California combined, only about 5 percent of it is cultivable. Packed into the fertile Nile valley and its delta are more than 30 million people and the population continues to grow.

The other major Arab countries in Africa are the Sudan, lying south of Egypt, and the North African states of Libya, Tunisia, Algeria, and Morocco. Each is a relatively important country in its own right, but none plays a decisive role in the Palestine conflict.

The chief contribution of oil-rich Libya is to give money to Egypt, to help compensate the UAR for revenue lost through the closing of the Suez Canal since the 1967 Middle Eastern war. Kuwait and Saudi Arabia also dip into their oil earnings to help Egypt.

Tunisia, Algeria, and Morocco all gained their independence from France, but are strikingly different from one another. Tunisia, under the strict but rational leadership of President Habib Bourguiba, is relatively relaxed in its attitude toward Israel. Algeria, led by President Houari Boumedienne, a socialist former army officer, breathes verbal fire against the Jewish state, but is separated by many hundreds of miles from Israel. King Hassan of Morocco, who survived an attempted coup d'état by Moroccan army officers in 1971, is preoccupied by internal political and economic problems.

These many Arab states range from socialist regimes, often led by soldiers, as in the Sudan, Libya, and Algeria, to the monarchies of Morocco, Jordan, and Saudi Arabia. To strengthen cooperation among these disparate entities, Egypt in 1945 took the lead in creating the Arab League, a body designed to coordinate Arab policies. Former French colonies joined the Arab League, as they became independent. Headquarters of the League is Cairo, reflecting the status of the UAR as the most important Arab state.

One ambitious effort of the Arab League was to organize an economic boycott of Israel. A boycott office was established in Damascus, with branches in other Arab capitals. Foreign companies were threatened with loss of Arab business if they traded with Israel. A number of European and American firms stopped doing business with the Zionist state rather than lose their Arab trade. Ships which carried cargoes for Israel were blacklisted in Arab ports.

In the early years of statehood, when both the Suez Canal and the Strait of Tiran were closed to Israeli shipping, the boycott did some damage to the Israeli economy by forcing the Jewish state to go far afield to acquire some essentials. Israel, for example, had to buy petroleum from Venezuela, despite the proximity of Middle Eastern oil. Now, however, Iran ships oil to Israel through the Strait of Tiran. Although the Arab boycott remains in force, it represents only a pinprick to the Israeli economy, which has greatly expanded its trade with West Africa, eastern Europe, the Common Market, and the United States.

Over the years some Arab leaders have tried to federate various Arab states. One such plan, the abortive Egyptian-Syrian union, has been mentioned. Another was an effort by King Abdullah to group Syria, Jordan, Palestine, and Iraq in a Greater Syria, under his rule. This never came to pass and, indeed, tribal and political rivalries have doomed all efforts to merge major Arab countries.

In 1971 the UAR, Syria, and Libya formed a loose union called the Federation of Arab Republics. The Sudan has signaled its intention to join. Ultimately the new union is scheduled to have a common flag and anthem. Nonetheless, each member of the federation retains its national sovereignty and it remains to be seen how closely the partners coordinate their domestic and foreign policies. Egypt, as a result of the federation, changed its name to the Arab Republic of Egypt.

A relatively new phenomenon is the emergence of Arab commando groups, organized more formally than the fedayeen who used to raid Israel from Jordan and the Gaza Strip. More than ten such guerrilla groups operate from bases in Lebanon, Syria, and Jordan against Israel. The most important commando organization is Al Fatah, headed by Yasir Arafat.

The Arabs most directly affected by the creation of Israel were the Palestinians, particularly those who became refugees. Yet from 1948 until 1967 the Arab struggle against Israel was conducted by other Arab governments and armies, acting in the name of the Palestinians. The Six Day War proved conclusively that Arab armies were no match for Israel, and Yasir Arafat, among others, decided that the Palestinians must take matters into their own hands.

Arafat's answer was to arm and train young guerrillas for harassing operations against Israel, with the ultimate aim of eradicating the Jewish state. The proliferation of commando groups resulted from differing political views among guerrilla leaders as to what kind of Palestinian entity should replace Israel. The organizations loosely group themselves under Arafat's leadership, but in fact each unit operates mostly on its own.

The rise of these bodies of armed men embarrassed their Arab host governments. Public opinion and allegiance to the Palestine cause forced the governments of Lebanon, Syria, and Jordan to permit the commandos to operate from bases on their soil. Their activities, however, brought punishing counter raids by the Israeli army.

The bulk of commando forces are based in Jordan, where for a time they virtually shared rule of the country with King Hussein. In 1970, however, the king ordered the Jordan army to drive the guerrillas from Jordanian towns back to their desert bases. A series of bloody fights gave the upper hand to King Hussein, but lost him much support throughout the Arab world.

Israeli defense minister Moshe Dayan discounts the ability of the commandos to hamper Israeli administration of the oc-

Israeli defense minister Moshe Dayan.

cupied zones. In July 1971, following an outbreak of fighting between guerrillas and the Jordan army, a number of Arab commandos crossed the frontier and surrendered to Israel. They claimed to prefer arrest by the Israelis to the treatment they were receiving from King Hussein's tough Bedouin soldiers.

Examining the relations between Israel and its immediate Arab neighbors, one might conclude there is little hope of reconciliation between these two Semitic contestants for the land of Palestine. Arab governments now press two sets of demands on the Jewish state—a rollback from territories occupied in 1967 and, once that is done, a settlement of the Palestine refugee problem, created in 1948.

Other thorny issues exist, including division of Jordan River waters, on which not only Israel, but Lebanon, Syria, and Jordan depend in varying degree for irrigation of their farmlands. In 1953, to bring water to its Negev desert, Israel began work on a water-diversion canal at the B'not Yaakov bridge on the Jordan River, between Lake Huleh and the Sea of Galilee.

Because this work fell within a demilitarized zone established between Israel and Syria, the latter obtained a United Nations stop-work order against Israel. Jewish workmen left the B'not Yaakov site, but only after the United States had put pressure on Israel by temporarily cutting off economic aid.

President Eisenhower then sent Eric Johnston as a special envoy to the Middle East, to negotiate a compromise settlement of the Jordan River dispute. Johnston worked out a formula, which would have allocated 60 percent of Jordan River waters to Lebanon, Syria, and Jordan and 40 percent to Israel. Engineers on both sides agreed to the compromise. But Arab governments refused to accept any sharing of the historic river with Israel.

Meanwhile, Israeli engineers switched their diversion point from B'not Yaakov to a place just north of the Sea of Galilee and wholly within the Jewish state. Work was completed on a

108-inch concrete pipeline, designed to carry river water south to the parched Negev.

In 1959 the Israeli government expressed alarm at the rate at which the nation's water table was falling. Promising to use only that amount of water awarded to the Jews under the Johnston Plan, Israel turned the taps, and Jordan River water began to flow southward through the huge pipeline to the Negev, opening fresh lands for settlement of immigrants.

The Jordan River dispute illustrates how, at almost every point, Arab and Israeli interests seem to collide. Yet, dark as this background is, significant changes in day-to-day Arab-Jewish relations are being wrought in two areas captured by the Israeli army in 1967. These places are the city of Jerusalem and the West Bank of Jordan.

One bright winter day early in 1971 I stood at the Wailing Wall, inside the walls of the Old City of Jerusalem. Before

At the Wailing Wall, inside the walls of the Old City of Jerusalem.
(K. Meyerowitz)

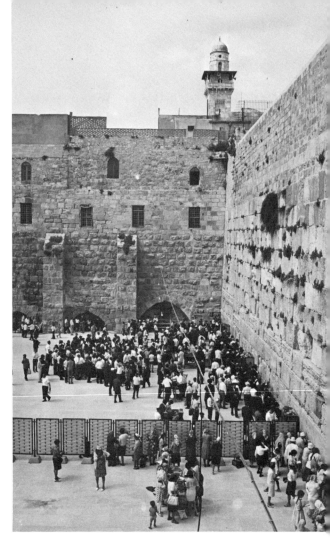

A screen at the Wailing Wall separates the sections for men and women.

1967 the line between Jordan and Israel had cut through the middle of Jerusalem. The Old City, including the Wailing Wall, had belonged to Jordan. Now it was possible to go unhindered from the western part of Jerusalem, which had been in Israel, through the gates of the Old City to the Wailing Wall. The sky was blue, and sunlight turned to honey color the old moss-tufted stones of the mighty wall, built by the Jews under King Herod two thousand years ago. Jewish men and boys, some dressed in black, with ringlets of hair falling down their cheeks, swayed at their prayers before the wall. On the other side of a separating screen Jewish women prayed at their section of the wall.

Suddenly a raucous noise filled the air around the worshippers. It was the recorded voice of an Arab *muezzin*, summoning the Moslem faithful to noonday prayers. In former, less sophisticated, days, muezzins used to climb the tall minarets of mosques, place cupped hands to their mouths, and ring out the melodious Arabic words, handed down to Moslems from the days of Mohammed the Prophet. Now, almost universally throughout the Arab world, the call is recorded and amplified through loudspeakers mounted on the minarets. So it was that day at the Wailing Wall in Jerusalem, where Arabs and Jews prayed side by side, as it were, in a place holy to them both.

Here on Mount Moriah, in the center of Jerusalem, Abraham, the "friend of God," had prepared to sacrifice his son Isaac. Solomon built the Jewish Temple on this site, and centuries later, at the time of Jesus, King Herod rebuilt its walls. All that remains of the ancient temple is Herod's Western Wall, popularly known as the Wailing Wall. From this wall, Jews are told by their Talmud, the divine spirit never departed.

When the Arabs conquered Jerusalem in the seventh century A.D., the temple site became holy to Moslems as well. Here, from the very rock where Abraham and Isaac had stood, Mohammed, riding his horse el-Burak, is said to have been carried to heaven. The Mosque of Omar, also called Dome of the Rock, celebrates this event. Inside the spacious mosque visitors look upon the rock associated with Abraham, Isaac, and Mohammed. Mount Moriah is to Moslems the third most sacred place on earth, after Mecca and Medina in Arabia.

From ancient times that part of Jerusalem near the temple site has been called the Jewish Quarter. Since the Six Day War the municipal government of Jerusalem has been rebuilding the Jewish Quarter and also, through excavation, bringing to light the lower layers of Herod's wall. Many of the skilled stonemasons at work in the Old City, however, do not wear the *kipa,* or Jewish skullcap. They wear the flowing *keffiyah* and *agal*—a kind of shawl worn over the head, held in place by a cloth band—for they are Arabs.

Arab and Jew, working together. The significance of this can be appreciated by anyone who knew Jerusalem before the 1967 war, when an ugly slash of no-man's-land divided the Holy City, with hostile Jordanian and Israeli troops manning the ramparts on either side. During the brief but bitter fighting in 1967, Israeli troops drove Jordan's Arab Legion not only from the Old City walls, but from all lands west of the Jordan River.

For the first time since the creation of the State of Israel in 1948, Jerusalem was united. The Wailing Wall again belonged to Jews. Swiftly the Knesset passed a law declaring the city a united whole. The 70,000 Arabs of the Old City, or East Jerusalem, as Israelis call it, were given special identity cards, describing them as "permanent residents" of the Jewish state. This status allows Jerusalem's Arabs to travel freely throughout Israel. They receive Israeli social welfare payments and, equally important, the same wages paid to Jewish workers.

"By any objective measurement most Arabs of East Jerusalem are better off today than they were under Jordan." Speaking was Maron Ben-Venisti, the Jewish official in charge of East Jerusalem affairs in the city administration of Mayor Teddy Kollek. Mr. Ben-Venisti was describing Israeli wages and social security benefits—both much higher than the Arabs of the Old City had received from Jordan before 1967.

Prior to the 1967 war, said Mr. Ben-Venisti, there had been a 6 to 8 percent unemployment rate among Arabs in the Old City. Now, thanks to a massive building program sponsored by the Israeli government, there was a labor shortage in the Holy City. The minimum wage paid to unskilled workers, whether Arab or Jewish, is just under 400 Israeli pounds monthly, or about $110. Under Jordanian rule the minimum wage had been

The Old City of Jerusalem. The Jaffa Gate is in the foreground and the Mosque of Omar (Dome of the Rock) in the center background. (Israel Government Tourist Office

The wall which cut Jerusalem in two before the Israeli army in 1967 conquered Old Jerusalem and unified the city. (Zev Radovan)

the equivalent of 92 Israeli pounds. "Even allowing for a 50 percent increase in the cost of living," remarked Mr. Ben-Venisti, "there has been a real rise in Arab income."

Outside Jerusalem lie the towns, villages, and countryside of the West Bank, that portion of Palestine which was annexed to the Hashemite Kingdom of Jordan by King Abdullah in 1949 and which is now occupied by Israel. Living on the West Bank, as we have noted, are 599,000 Arabs. They remain citizens of Jordan and, unlike the Arabs of Old Jerusalem, are not classified as permanent residents of Israel. But these hundreds of thousands of Palestine Arabs, too, are deeply affected by the Jewish occupation.

More than 30,000 West Bank Arabs commute to Israel to work. They earn 17 Israeli pounds daily (almost $5) for unskilled labor, up to 40 pounds for skilled work. Social security benefits are laid aside for them. They work in the Haifa shipyard and on construction projects throughout Israel. If the commuting distance is too great, they sleep near their work and return to the West Bank on weekends.

An elderly Arab in a stone-quarrying village on the West Bank told me that since the Israelis had come there had been a rising demand for the buff- and pink-colored building stone of his district. Arab farmers often send their crops in Israeli trucks to Jewish markets in Tel Aviv, Jerusalem, and Haifa. Many of Israel's "own" Arabs, who have been citizens of the Jewish state since 1948, hold jobs at relatively sophisticated levels in Israeli cities and towns. These people, an expert told me, now were importing West Bank Arabs to do their "village chores."

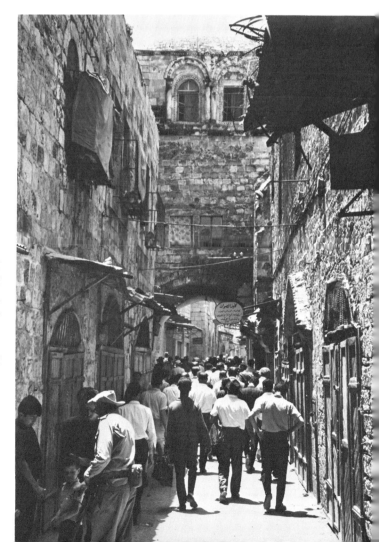

The busy, crowded streets of the Old City of Jerusalem echo to the steps of Christian, Jewish, and Moslem pilgrims. (Israel Government Tourist Office)

Driving through the West Bank, one sees miles of water pipelines glinting in the sunlight, snaking across the stony hills and fields. These pipelines, installed by Jewish engineers, are giving many Arab villages a sustained water supply for the first time. Some village councils have obtained Israeli loans to bring in electricity. The Arab villagers themselves, through local taxes, pay for some of these benefits. But a large share of the cost is borne by Israel.

What do these examples of day-to-day cooperation mean for the future? Does this intermingling in Jerusalem and on the West Bank point the way to eventual Arab-Jewish reconciliation? Israelis would like to believe so. But few are optimistic.

"Privately," declared a professor at the Hebrew University in Jerusalem, "some Arabs will admit they never had it so good. But none will speak openly of cooperation."

Arab refugees in the old Jewish quarter in Jerusalem. (*United Nations*)

An Orthodox Jew chats with an Arab juice seller in Jerusalem. The juice is called tamarandy, *made from dates of palm trees.*
(Zev Radovan)

A distinguished Israeli politician, who speaks fluent Arabic, shook his head when asked about a possible Arab change of heart.

"Why should an Arab of Nablus accept Jewish rule over Nablus, even if his wages have increased threefold?" he asked. (Nablus is an Arab town on the West Bank.)

"A liberal Israeli policy," the politician continued, "can change the *behavior* of Arabs living under occupation, but not their *aims*. Their national aspiration remains, understandably, Arab government of Arab peoples and Arab territories."

One day I visited an Arab secondary school in a West Bank town. The director of the school was a tall young Arab, a Christian, with a doctoral degree from the American University of Beirut. In fluent English he expressed his bitter feelings about the Israelis.

"We live at different paces, Arabs and Jews," declared the teacher. "I do not want to see a skyscraper springing up beside my house. If I want to raise olive trees on my land, why should I be told that I should grow strawberries, even if it is more profitable?"

This educated man had chosen, it would seem to an outsider, two ill-matched complaints. Olive growing is extensive agriculture, requiring much land for a modest return. Israeli experts have persuaded a number of West Bank farmers to switch from olive trees to strawberries. Their fruit, flown to European markets by Jewish exporters, yields a handsome profit.

The Arab school director, well-to-do by West Bank standards, did not himself grow olives. Could he really speak for West Bank farmers? "Resist, resist the Israelis," was the message this Christian Arab teacher was pounding home to the high school Arab boys he directed. These young men would not go out to till the fields, but would take white collar and professional jobs. The teacher, and the boys he influenced, were leading very different lives from the Arab peasants, whose strawberry crops were bringing benefits their families never had enjoyed before.

"Man," emphasized the teacher, "does not live by bread alone." He went on to explain what he meant. His opposition to the Israeli occupation was based on the right of Palestine Arabs to govern themselves and develop their lands in the way they saw fit. Economic benefits which the occupation might bring did not erase the stigma of being controlled by conquering Jews.

I came away from our talk with an unanswered question. To what extent would poor Arabs, more prosperous under the Israelis than they had been under Jordanian rule, agree with the western-educated teacher? Many Israeli officials cling to the hope that economic betterment will help to change Arab attitudes, at least on the West Bank.

When he talked about skyscrapers, the school director was on surer ground. After the Six Day War the Israeli government not only had unified Jerusalem but had incorporated large tracts of surrounding Arab lands inside the city limits of "greater Jerusalem." Clusters of high-rise apartment houses were springing up on some of the stony hills outside the city, radically changing the eastern approach to Jerusalem.

West Bank Arabs resented two things about this development—first, that the city limits were expanded by decree, and, second, that within this greater Jerusalem Israel was building blocks of flats for Jewish settlers. Not only Arabs, but many other people to whom Jerusalem is meaningful, regretted that the outskirts of the Holy City were taking on a starkly modern look and that Israel unilaterally was predetermining the future of the city.

There is a fundamental difference in Israeli and Arab attitudes toward Jerusalem and toward the West Bank as a whole. Most Israelis, given stable peace conditions between Arab nations and themselves, are ready to cede the West Bank to an Arab authority—either to King Hussein or to a Palestine Arab ad-

A street scene in a West Bank town, where Arabs and Jews mingle.

ministration. Arabs living on the West Bank are convinced that, sooner or later, their lands again will belong to them, either as an independent Palestinian state or as part of the Hashemite Kingdom of Jordan.

But the 70,000 Arabs of Jerusalem have no such assurance. Both the Israeli government and the Knesset have stressed that the unified city will remain within Israel, as capital of the Jewish state. No matter what peace settlement is achieved, the Old City will not be given back to the Arabs, so far as Israel is concerned.

"Our aim after the June war," declared Mr. Ben-Venisti, "was to integrate the Old City with a minimum of tension, but at the same time to show enough firmness to convince the Arabs that the present situation would be lasting."

By "present situation" the Israeli official meant a unified Jerusalem, with "its essential Jewish character preserved." Seventy-five percent of the unified city's population, he stressed, was Jewish. The other quarter was Arab.

Essentially, Israel's building plans call for constructing four complexes of apartment buildings on former Jordanian land surrounding Jerusalem. These housing units, designed to accommodate 122,000 residents, will be occupied primarily by Jews. Israeli Housing Minister Zev Sharef bluntly ascribed a political purpose to the building program—to settle as many Jews as possible within greater Jerusalem and thus emphasize the Jewish character of the city. New housing for Arabs also would be built, but near the West Bank cities of Bethlehem and Ramallah.

On February 16, 1971, the United States Department of State sharply criticized Israel's construction plans as "unacceptable." The American government held that the final status of Jerusalem must await agreement between Jordan and Israel, taking into consideration the interests of the international community.

Many Israelis are willing to concede some form of international control over Moslem mosques and Christian churches within Jerusalem. But they are adamant that political control of the Holy City should remain in Israeli hands. This point of view was rejected by every Arab to whom I spoke, both on the West Bank and in Jerusalem. All insisted that, as part of a peace package, the Old City must return to the Arabs.

Faced with this attitude, Mayor Kollek, Mr. Ben-Venisti, and other Israelis proceed with caution in their personal and official relationships with Arabs. "Our goals are limited," said one high-ranking Jewish official. "We are not trying to change the political loyalty of Jerusalem Arabs. We know we cannot."

Mr. Ben-Venisti put it another way. "We have a *negative* goal. We tell the Arabs—do not create trouble, do not collaborate with terrorists. Beyond that, we do not try to force their cooperation."

Arabs refused to stand for election to the Jerusalem city council after 1967, with the result that all thirty-one members of Mayor Kollek's council are Jewish. Yet, said Mr. Ben-Venisti, five hundred Arab municipal workers of the former Jordanian administration in the Old City had stayed at their jobs and now worked for Israel. They did not appear to regard this as collaboration.

Eighty-five percent of all policemen serving in East Jerusalem were Arab, he continued. More than one hundred Arab policemen had been recruited and trained by Israel. "And a Jewish Israeli," declared Mr. Ben-Venisti, "is required to obey them, just as he would obey a Jewish policeman.

"We recognize," said Ben-Venisti, "that Arab municipal officials stand in a cross fire. We do not want them to be called collaborators. If a tense situation develops," he went on, "I do not send in my Arab assistant. I go myself. He knows I will not put him in a position where he can be accused of collaboration."

But what did his assistant, and other Jerusalem Arabs, really think of all this? Mr. Ben-Venisti paused.

"We do not explore each other's thinking," he replied. "If I know my assistant hates me, I have to act." Arabs and Jews, he added, had to coexist side by side, whether they liked it or not. "Sometimes," he said, "it is better not to know exactly what the other one is thinking."

In summary, the West Bank seems to offer the best hope of potential cooperation between Arabs and Jews, once peace is achieved. Thousands of West Bank Arabs know they can earn a better living through association with Israel, either by working directly for Jewish employers or by marketing their produce through Israel. But the latter's tough determination to hold Old Jerusalem, and to change its character, may erode whatever confidence West Bank Arabs might build up in their Jewish neighbor.

Even at best, the people of the West Bank cannot make peace with Israel on their own. They must await the leadership of established Arab governments. The obvious peacemaker, from the West Bank point of view, is King Hussein. But the security of the young monarch's throne is threatened by the Palestine Arab commando movement within Jordan, which would like a government without Hussein as king. Hussein may be able to keep Arab extremists in check and hold his throne. But he is not strong enough to risk commando and general Arab anger by making a separate peace with Israel.

The key to the future seems to lie with Egypt, the most populous Arab state and by far the most powerful militarily. If Egyptian President Anwar el-Sadat, successor to the late President Nasser, felt it possible to live at peace with the Jewish state, other Arab countries would follow suit—some willingly, like Lebanon; others perhaps resentfully, like Syria and Iraq.

To satisfy Egypt, Israel must withdraw from the bulk of the Sinai Peninsula, including Sharm el-Sheikh at the southern tip, which commands the entry to the Strait of Tiran and the Israeli port of Eilat. Between them Israel and Egypt must agree on the future of the Gaza Strip, a green oasis desperately overcrowded with bitter, unemployed Arabs.

If Israel's tanks and soldiers were to withdraw from Sinai, Egypt says, it would reopen the Suez Canal and allow Israeli shipping to pass through the canal and the Strait of Tiran. The canal, blocked by scuttled vessels, is closed to all shipping. The Strait of Tiran currently is in Israeli hands. Israel so far has refused to retreat, pending ironclad guarantees of peaceful coexistence, including unhindered passage through Middle Eastern waterways for Israeli ships. All this, the Israeli government insists, should be confirmed through a formal peace treaty, negotiated directly between Israel and Egypt.

Next in line with complaints against Israel stands Jordan. King Hussein wants back the West Bank and East Jerusalem. The former he may get; the latter he will not, if Israelis have their way.

Syria's quarrel with Israel—control of the Golan Heights —possibly could be settled by demilitarizing the area and putting it under international supervision.

Settlement of all these disputes would clear the way to consider a long-standing Arab demand—that all Arab refugees be given a free choice of returning to their Palestine homes or being compensated for their loss. This demand is rooted in UN General Assembly resolution 194/III of 1948, which states that "refugees wishing to return to their homes and live at peace with their neighbors should be permitted to do so at the earliest practicable date, and that compensation should be paid for property of those choosing not to return."

On June 29, 1971, the Israeli government offered to recompense Arab residents of the Old City of Jerusalem for property they once had owned in what is now Israel. An estimated 10,000 Old City Arabs owned land or houses in Jaffa, West Jerusalem, and other Palestinian towns prior to 1948. Israel now proposes to pay them for their lost holdings. This would put the "permanent residents" of the Old City on the same footing as Israeli Arabs—those who did not flee from their homes in

1948–who long ago were offered compensation for any property they lost when Israel became a state.

Israeli officials noted that 80 percent of Israeli Arabs had accepted money for their lost property. The hope is that many Arabs of the Old City of Jerusalem will do the same.

The new offer, explained Yakov S. Shapiro, Israeli minister of justice, did not apply to Arabs of the West Bank, the Gaza Strip, and other occupied territories. These lands had not been incorporated into Israel, as East Jerusalem had been, and thus did not fall within the jurisdiction of Israeli law.

Through natural increase of the 1948 refugee population, plus the flight of thousands of Arabs after the 1967 war, the number of uprooted and homeless Palestine Arabs now living as refugees in other Arab lands has swollen to more than one million. From the teeming camps in which these people live have sprung the Arab commando organizations, whose primary goal is eradication of the Jewish state.

In 1968 two professors of the American University of Beirut interviewed 122 typical refugee families, comprising 800 individuals, asking them whether they would return to Palestine if they could. This study disclosed that 64 percent of the 1948 refugees and 82 percent of the 1967 refugees wanted to go back. Only 15 percent of the earlier refugee population and 2 percent of the 1967 group voted against return to Palestine.

Since 1948 Israel has taken back fewer than 100,000 Arab refugees, mostly under family reunion plans. Israel refuses to accept more, charging that many of the refugees fled in 1948 at the urging of their own Arab leaders. Beyond this, the Zionist state is committed to "ingather" Jews from throughout the world, and, the Israelis claim, there is not enough room to accommodate both the Jewish immigrants and a great influx of Arab refugees.

The Law of Return, passed by the Knesset at the beginning of statehood, provides that "every Jew has a right to immigrate to Israel." In 1961 the Knesset passed a law forbidding a mass return of Arab refugees and stating that the only solution lay in the settlement of these people in Arab lands.

In 1947 Arab governments had rejected the UN partition plan, which laid the foundation of the Jewish state in Palestine. After the 1948 war the Arabs modified their stand. They demanded that Israel give back only those lands in excess of the territory assigned to the Jewish state by the partition plan. We recall that during the 1948 fighting Israel increased its assigned territory by more than 30 percent.

The 1967 Arab-Jewish war, bringing in its train additional Israeli expansion, modified even this Arab demand. Now Arab governments require that Israel roll itself back to its pre-1967 boundaries. The assumption is that if Israel were to do this, Arab regimes no longer would press for a further shrinkage of the Jewish state back to the earlier partition plan frontiers.

All this indicates that eventual concord between Arabs and Jews will require peeling off layer after layer of old grievances. The West Bank, where today Arabs and Jews have no choice but to intermingle, provides a glimmer of hope that one day these Semitic cousins might dwell together in peace.

7

Who Is a Jew?

Everywhere one sees them in Israel—small dark men, working often at construction sites or at menial labor. They are not Arabs, but "oriental" Jews—that is, Jewish immigrants to Israel from countries other than Europe or the Americas. Morocco, Yemen, Iraq, Egypt, and other Arab and Asian countries were their homelands before they came to Israel.

During the British mandate Jewish immigration to Palestine was overwhelmingly European in origin. From 1919 until May 1948, when the State of Israel was founded, 89.6 percent of all Jewish immigrants came from Europe, America, and Oceania (Australia and New Zealand). Only 10.4 percent hailed from Africa and Asia.

After the first Arab-Jewish war the scales tipped the other way. Formerly friendly Arab lands now became hostile to Jews and either expelled them or made life so uncomfortable that they preferred to leave. Between 1948 and 1971 more than half a million of these so-called oriental Jews found their way to Israel.

More than half of all Jewish immigrants since 1948 have come from Africa and Asia.

Under the Law of Return, oriental Jews have the same right to be "ingathered" to Israel as Jews from western lands. But their cultural background and level of education are often very different from those of Israeli immigrants from the United States, Britain, or even Poland and the Soviet Union. The result is social tension—obscured in part by the overriding preoccupation of all Israelis with defense, but nonetheless there, below the surface. "All Jews in Israel have the same *rights*," declared one official, "but not the same *possibilities*."

Up to 10 percent of the Israeli population, at a conservative estimate, lives below the poverty line, defined as a monthly income of 70 Israeli pounds per person, or 20 dollars. A majority of these people are oriental Jews, often with five or more children. European Jews usually have smaller families. The Israelis living at poverty level tend to feel discriminated against—and they

A Yemenite goldsmith in Israel. (Israel Government Tourist Office)

An elderly Jew in Jerusalem. (K. Meyerowitz)

are, in the sense that their lack of education deprives them of equal opportunity to compete with European Jews for jobs.

All Israeli children have similar schooling. "But," remarked a distinguished European Jew, "my son comes home to educated parents and a home full of books. His oriental friend may be just as bright. But he goes home to a culturally deprived family, with few books."

A partial answer is to "pump more education into such children," as one expert put it, in the form of tutors, longer school hours, special courses. "But," the expert added, "it takes a generation or more for such people to catch up after centuries of deprivation," particularly since the level of education among Israelis of western origin is extremely high.

"I would not compare our social tension to the Negro-white conflict in the United States," declared an Israeli official, "not at all. Ours is the sociological problem of people who have come from entirely different cultural backgrounds."

He referred to the situation in Britain, where, he asserted, "if someone comes from the lower social strata, he must have great talent to break through. The problem is more complicated in Israel, because our people came from many different countries."

"Social tension is confined largely to newcomers," claimed Gideon Hausner, the lawyer who successfully prosecuted the Nazi criminal Adolf Eichmann, and who is now legal adviser to the Israeli government. "Older oriental residents, and especially their children born here, are indistinguishable from European Jews, except in the pronunciation of certain words."

Mixed oriental-European marriages are taking place, particularly between *sabras,* or Jews born in Israel. This further blurs the distinction between differing backgrounds. Many Jews of oriental extraction have risen high in Israel. They hold important government and army posts and are members of the Knesset, though not yet in proportion to the number of oriental Jews in the country. Others are doctors, lawyers, writers.

The great need, as most Israelis see it, is to integrate oriental newcomers before any sense of discrimination they may feel hardens. The supreme instrument of integration is the Israeli army, through which funnels almost every Jewish citizen in the country. At the age of eighteen boys serve for three years, girls for twenty months. Girls may be excused from military service on religious grounds, but not young men. Married women also do not serve.

The army, declared Brigadier General Yizhak Arad, chief education officer, is the great leveler where every Israeli Jew, whether from Morocco or the United States, "gets a chance at equal competition."

The army, quite apart from military training, conducts a detailed program of education for all recruits. Some oriental Jewish newcomers, explained General Arad, do not speak Hebrew—Israel's national language—on arrival. Once in the army, such recruits take an intensive course in Hebrew, within their units or at an area command school, depending on their proficiency.

Israeli soldiers. The Israeli army provides a detailed program of education as well as military training for all recruits. (Sommer Erich)

The next step is to insure that every soldier, by the time he returns to civilian life, has a primary school certificate covering eight years of schooling. Soldiers who do not have their certificates, said General Arad, attend a three-month course at the Marcus School on Mount Carmel, near Haifa.

Ninety percent of the students there, most of whom are oriental Jews, get their certificate after three intensive months at Marcus, where two teachers work with each small group. Many such boys, the general remarked, ask for permission to study four additional months at Marcus, to get a ten-year equivalency certificate qualifying them for vocational training. If they want to go even further and acquire a secondary school diploma, corre-

An Israeli woman soldier teaches school in a border village.

sponding to that of an American high school, soldiers study evenings or through correspondence courses in the civilian school system. The army pays the bills.

"Most students at Israeli universities," remarked General Arad, "are European Jews. Entry is competitive and western-trained Jews naturally have an advantage. With university cooperation, we select oriental soldiers for one year of special studies within the army. Each year," he added, "about 120 such soldiers go on to university."

All soldiers, regardless of background, learn Jewish history and hear lectures about the Israeli state in which they live. Moroccan, Iraqi, Yemenite, and other so-called oriental Jews are also told what special contributions their communities have made to Jewish tradition and culture over the centuries.

"Many oriental Jews," concluded General Arad, "tend to cluster among their own kind in civilian life. So the army is their first real melting pot." Often, he said, oriental Jews who had gone through army training broke out of this type of self-imposed "ghetto" when they returned to civilian status.

Many experts claim that social tensions are less acute today than in the 1950s, largely because the nation has a greater percentage of sabras. In 1969 the Jewish population of Israel (excluding the Arabs) was divided into 1,125,000 native sabras and 1,375,000 million Jews born abroad. Of the latter, 315,000 Jews were born in Asia, 355,000 came from Africa, and 702,000 from Europe and America.

Looked at another way, Israel's Jewish population today is 45 percent native-born. Those born abroad are split almost equally between European and oriental Jews.

"We have two currents at work here," explained an Israeli. "The orientals have more children, so their percentage of the population may increase. But sabras, having been exposed only to Israeli schools and to the Israeli army, and not to foreign cultures, feel less oriental-European distinction than their parents did."

These same experts acknowledge that in some ways Israel's social tensions are more visible today than in the past. Groups of young oriental Jews, calling themselves "Black Panthers," roam city streets at night, particularly in Jerusalem, and clash occasionally with police. These gangs of long-haired youths form a small minority of Israel's oriental Jewish population. But they express, in bitterness and violence, the conviction of many of their class that they are treated as second-class citizens.

Oriental Jews want to end what they regard as discrimination and to gain job and social opportunities equal to those enjoyed by European Jews. The latter see the problem in another dimension. They, too, want to eliminate the stigma of second-class citizenship from their non-European brethren. But west-

ern-trained Israelis hope to accomplish this by shaping the outlook of Jews from Asia and Africa toward the European
standards from which western Zionists sprang. Israel, in the view
of its European and American settlers—who still dominate political, economic, and cultural life in the country—should exhibit a
European character and not become "Levantine," or eastern
Mediterranean, in culture.

A sense of Jewish unity fostered by Arab hostility, especially since the Six Day War, tends to paper over these internal
social conflicts, except for the outbursts of angry young people
like the "Black Panthers." But the tensions are there and Israeli
experts expect them to surface more strongly, if and when attention can be diverted from the external Arab threat.

Underlying all this is a gradual shift of power from older
Russian, Polish, German, and other European Zionists, who came
to Palestine as settlers, to sabras born in the promised land. The
latter, many of whom speak Arabic and count Israeli Arabs
among their friends, tend to be more understanding of the root
causes of Arab fear and enmity than do some of the earlier generations of Zionists.

This conflict of generations will not be fought out in the
streets but within the political parties and Histadrut. Many sabras, born of European parents, adhere as devotedly as do their
elders to European standards of education and culture. But
younger Jews also tend to be more out-reaching to the Arabs,
both inside and outside Israel.

Another facet of Israeli life, the relationship between
church and state, affects all Israeli Jews, regardless of background and whether or not they are religious. To begin with,
only about 20 percent of Israeli Jews are "observant"—that is, attend synagogue and adhere to religious laws.

"Another 30 percent of Jews are believers and sympathetic," explained a prominent rabbi, "but do not go to synagogue." He paused for a moment. "Perhaps 90 percent of all

Israeli Jews have a positive attitude toward Judaism—that is, respect it."

A distinguished Jewish scholar, himself not religious, expressed it differently. "The past is ever present with us," he declared. "We Jews are in a permanent confrontation with all the ingredients of our past."

Judaism, the religion of the Jews, the scholar continued, was one aspect of that past—an essential part of Jewish civilization, but not the only part. Just as important to this man was a Jew's "way of daily life, his relationship to his family."

Zionism, in other words—a commitment to the return of the Jewish people to Palestine—is not necessarily synonymous with Judaism. "It is quite possible," affirmed a leading Israeli figure in public life, "to feel passionately a sense of Jewishness apart from Judaism. So we have a new definition of Jewishness." Or, he amended himself, Israelis were in the process of exploring a new definition. "It is easy to empty a vessel," he continued. "The problem is to fill it again. How does an irreligious Jew gain a new sense of Jewishness, based on ethics, not religion?"

Even among observant Jews there is great variety. At one extreme is Naturei Karta, a group of perhaps two hundred families, who refuse to pay taxes and do not recognize the State of Israel. These people are anti-Zionist, claiming that establishment of the State of Israel must await the coming of the Messiah.

Allied to this group but more numerous is Agudat Israel, an ultra-Orthodox religious community. Members of Agudat Israel accept the legitimacy of the state but demand that it be changed to a theocracy governed by the rabbinate, or Jewish clergy.

The great mass of religious Jews belong to the National Religious Party, a centrist group which does not call for a theocracy but favors greater rabbinical influence in the shaping of secular law. This party holds a significant bloc of Knesset seats and is represented in Israel's coalition government.

Moses, the great Jewish lawgiver, was both the religious and secular leader of the ancient Hebrews, in their long journey up out of Egypt and back to the promised land. The rules he laid down still form the foundation of Judaic religious observance. Israelis could not discard the Mosaic law and still preserve Jewish tradition. The result, in modern Israel, is compromise, with the religious minority in some ways imposing its will on the nonobservant majority.

All Israelis, for example, whether Jewish, Moslem, or Christian, eat *kosher* food when flying El Al, the national airline, or dining in government-owned restaurants. (Kosher food is prepared according to religious dietary laws.) All Israeli soldiers receive kosher food in the army, regardless of their personal attitude toward Judaism.

In deference to religious sentiment, no public transportation is supposed to operate on Saturday, the Jewish Sabbath. Even here there is a compromise, for the Haifa municipality voted to allow its buses to run on the Sabbath.

"What we have in Israel," declared a senior government official, "is a compromise in the area of church and state. This suits the needs of most of our citizens."

Gideon Hausner defined the Jewish nation as one "which does not start from scratch. We have a long tradition, to which the Jews owe their physical existence as a nation."

Without this tradition to support them and to unite them in spirit, Mr. Hausner meant, the Jews in their scattered Diaspora never would have survived as an identifiable people.

"The great majority of Israelis," he continued, "would like to see the values of our heritage adapted to the twentieth century."

But there is a problem. "Today's age is so innovative that the rabbis, as custodians of the heritage, are afraid to open the door even a little, lest winds of change sweep in. As a result, we are resolved to leave things to slow adaptation, in order not to cause a split within the nation. We want no head-on collision with the religious part of the community."

Israel, like Great Britain, has no written constitution. One reason is that Orthodox Jews, expressing themselves through the Chief Rabbinate, wanted Judaism to become the state religion, as Roman Catholicism is in Spain or Islam in Pakistan. The majority of Israelis would not accept this. So, in the spirit of compromise, the writing of a constitution was postponed.

The Knesset has a legal committee to draw up laws in draft form that are then presented to the parliament as a whole. Sitting on this committee, Mr. Hausner observed, is a rabbinical expert who explains what religious law has to say about the proposed legislation. "An attempt then is made," Mr. Hausner went on, "to adapt the religious law, if it is not too remote from our present-day needs.

"We are always casting about for ways," he emphasized, "to preserve the best we have, if we can live with it."

Judaic family law, he remarked, is stringent in application. He gave the example of a married man who dies, leaving behind a bachelor brother. Under the Mosaic code, the surviving man is supposed to marry his brother's widow. If he does not wish to do so, a ceremony can be performed that absolves him from this responsibility. But if the surviving brother is a minor, less than thirteen years old—the age at which a Jewish boy legally becomes a man—the widow is not permitted to remarry until the boy becomes thirteen and can decide what he wants to do.

The military rabbinate, Mr. Hausner went on, makes provision for frontline soldiers to deposit bills of divorcement from their wives. Then, if a soldier is killed, his wife is considered by law not a widow but a divorcee. She is legally free to remarry, and the dead soldier's brother has no encumbrance.

Jewish men named Cohen or derivatives of that name are regarded in Judaic tradition as belonging to priestly families. They are not allowed to marry divorced women. How, in the modern age, do Israelis named Cohen get around this stricture? "If a couple takes a trip and marries *outside* Israel," commented Mr. Hausner, "then the marriage is recognized as valid."

Judaic law regards marriage as a free contract between a man and woman—freely entered into, freely dissolved by mutual consent. Religious custom does not require, as western legal codes generally do, that one partner be found guilty in order for the other to obtain a divorce.

This Jewish procedure works in most cases of divorce, an expert said. But in those instances where there is not mutual agreement, Jewish religious law favors the husband. He is required to hand a bill of divorcement to his wife. If she refuses to accept it—"actually take the bill in her hands," a lawyer explained—then a rabbi must decide whether she is "guilty." If he judges her guilty and she still refuses to accept the bill of divorcement, the rabbi allows the man to marry another woman, without paying alimony to his first wife.

Ancient Jewish law, however, said nothing about a husband who, in one way or another, mistreated his wife and yet refused to give her a bill of divorcement. So the Israeli Knesset had to add something new to the body of law. Legislation was passed authorizing such a husband to be jailed if he declined to treat his wife fairly.

The above examples disclose a fundamental difference between Israeli and American legal systems. Israel has a normal structure of magistrates' courts, district courts, and Supreme Court to handle criminal and most other legal matters. But problems of marriage and divorce, or "personal status," fall within the jurisdiction of religious courts. This is true not only for Jewish Israelis, but for Moslem and Christian citizens as well. Each community goes to its own courts, where matters of personal status are decided according to the applicable religious codes. There is, for example, an Arab tribal court of three sheikhs which sits in

Beersheba, as well as other Moslem courts in communities where large numbers of Israeli Arabs live.

The task of fusing traditional Jewish law with modern practice has aroused controversy in Israel on one of the most fundamental questions of all—namely, who is a Jew? Religious law is clear on the point. Anyone born of a Jewish mother is a Jew. Whether or not that mother is an observant, or religious, Jew has nothing to do with the case. By contrast, a person born of a Jewish father and a non-Jewish mother is, according to rabbinical law, not a Jew.

In 1962 a Dominican priest named Oswald Rufeisin claimed the right to Israeli citizenship because his mother had been a Jew. According to religious law he was a Jew, though he belonged to a Roman Catholic order. His case went to the Supreme Court, which split on the issue. The majority ruled that Brother Rufeisin could not be accepted as a Jew because he professed another religion. Justice Haim Cohen wrote a minority brief that the government had no right to inquire into a man's religion. The upshot of the matter was that Brother Rufeisin, who still belongs to the Dominican order, became a *naturalized* Israeli citizen, not one by right of birth.

A second case had more profound meaning to a greater number of Israelis. A Jewish officer of the Israeli navy, Lieutenant Commander Benjamin Shalit, was married to an English Christian woman. Their children, therefore, were classified as non-Jewish by rabbinical law. The children were legally Israeli citizens, but Commander Shalit wanted them registered as *ethnically* Jewish. The Ministry of Interior refused his request, and Shalit went to court.

On January 23, 1970, the Supreme Court made a historic decision, by a 5-4 vote, that the child of a Jewish father and a non-Jewish mother had the right to be considered Jewish. The court ordered the Israeli government to register the Shalit chil-

Prime Minister Golda Meir.

dren as Jewish. The court's ruling appeared to mean that any person with at least one Jewish parent had the right to belong to *Le'um Hayehudi,* or "the Jewish people wherever they are."

A storm of protest broke out among religious Jews, partly on the grounds that the ruling would tend to encourage mixed marriages. Chief Rabbi Yitzhak Nissim, who led the fight to overturn the court's ruling, declared, "The Jewish people's nationhood is its religion and its religion is its nationality." The National Religious Party, headed by Interior Minister Moshe Shapiro, threatened to quit the coalition government led by Prime Minister Golda Meir.

The cabinet then wrote two key amendments to Israel's Law of Return, which were passed by the Knesset. A Jew, for the purposes of the Law of Return, was to be a person born of a Jewish mother who had not converted to another religion. The second amendment said that a non-Jew could acquire Jewish status by converting to Judaism. This second amendment also required that non-Jewish husbands and wives, and children of mixed marriages, should have the same legal rights as immigrating Jews.

These amendments nullified the Supreme Court ruling and, for the first time, wrote into civil law the rabbinical definition of who is a Jew. A counter-storm of protest now broke out, led by Israeli socialists and particularly by young people, advocating complete separation of church and state. Placards carried by demonstrators read "Democracy, not Theocracy," "Separate State from Religion," and "We are Jews of the twentieth century and not of the Egyptian Exodus."

To sum up, most Israelis agree that the great body of Jewish tradition, rooted in the teachings of Moses and the prophets, formed an essential link among Jews scattered throughout the world during the Diaspora. But the task of forging a modern State of Israel will require an adaptation that incorporates the best of Jewish tradition while discarding its anachronisms. Wisdom, ingenuity, and a spirit of compromise will be needed.

8

Guns, Butter, and Taxes

From the summer of 1967 through the end of 1970 almost
150,000 Jewish immigrants came to Israel, 17,000 of them from
the United States. In 1970 alone 40,000 newcomers arrived, far
above the average for the years preceding the Six Day War.
When the Jewish state is in trouble, when its existence appears
threatened, the tide of immigration swells, while the number of
dissatisfied Jews who leave Israel—for some do, every year—
declines. The influx of immigrants now has pushed the population of Israel above 3 million persons.

These 150,000 new arrivals since 1967 came to a land in
which housing was already short. Apartments had to be built for
them in towns and cities. Kibbutzim had to be founded and
equipment bought to stock new farms. Factories required expansion, schools and hospitals had to be constructed. All this came
under the heading of what Israelis call "settlement costs."

To absorb the newcomers, Israeli citizens dug deeper into
their own pockets. In 1970 Israel achieved the unenviable dis-

tinction of becoming the most heavily taxed nation in the world. "Thirty percent of my salary goes for income tax," a woman doctor told me. "When all other taxes are thrown in, I pay half my income to the state."

She shrugged and gestured around her small apartment. "My husband and I need a larger flat, now that the children are growing up. But we can't afford it."

Educationally and professionally this man and woman were at the top of the heap. Yet they could not accumulate capital. The more they earned, the more they were required to pay for the two great tasks confronting all Israelis—settlement of immigrants and defense.

To keep pace militarily with the Egyptians, Israel has ballooned its defense budget three to four times above pre-1967 levels. In 1970 the Jewish state spent $800 million to buy foreign arms, mostly aircraft and other equipment from the United States. Forty percent of the government's budget is devoted to security. One quarter of the Israeli labor force works in the defense effort, directly or indirectly.

To pay for all this the Israeli government in 1970 increased taxes of every kind: income taxes, corporation levies, the payments Israelis make to their national insurance plan. Government subsidies to families were reduced, except to those below the poverty line. Finally, the government slapped an additional 20 percent defense tax on all imports, except on essentials such as bread and rice.

To buy a new car which in the United States would sell for $3,000 an Israeli must pay about $12,000. The price of the car, in other words, is multiplied roughly four times to cover all import duties and taxes. A Volkswagen in Israel costs about what a Mercedes Benz or a Cadillac does in the United States.

Still Israel cannot pay its bills from its own resources alone. The state has to import capital from abroad, as it has done ever since 1948. In 1970 Israel suffered a balance of payments deficit of $1.3 billion, an enormous amount of red ink for such a small nation. This means that Israel imported goods that cost $1.3 billion dollars more than Israelis could earn by selling their own goods and services abroad.

In 1969 Israel reduced its deficit by borrowing increased amounts of money from governments and institutions abroad. In 1971 the nation's foreign debts stood close to $3 billion. Sixteen percent of the government's annual budget goes to debt repayment.

The nation's economic plight would indeed be desperate if it were not for two major sources of money flowing in from overseas. One of these, reparations from West Germany, amounts to $180 million yearly. Even larger are contributions from world Jewry, mostly in the United States. Israel counts on receiving about $600 million each year in the form of donations and German restitutions.

The latter began in 1952, when Chancellor Konrad Adenauer of West Germany and Foreign Minister Moshe Sharett of Israel signed an agreement in Luxembourg. This provided for the Federal Republic of Germany to pay the State of Israel $862 million, divided into fourteen yearly installments. The money was used to buy many kinds of German goods—iron, steel, finished steel products, chemicals, farm products—and send them to Israel.

Dr. Adenauer, a stern, aloof man who had been mayor of Cologne when the Nazis came to power, was an opponent of Hitler from the beginning. Removed from his office by the Nazis, Adenauer was under arrest or surveillance during much of Hitler's Third Reich. In 1949, when the victorious Allies allowed the West Germans to form a postwar government, Adenauer became the first chancellor, or prime minister.

He knew, as did most Germans, that money could not compensate for the slaughter by the Nazis of 6 million Jews. But Adenauer was determined that West Germans should do as much as possible to help the infant Jewish state. The Luxembourg Agreement expired March 31, 1966, and since that time West Germany has continued to give economic aid to Israel at the rate of about $30 million each year. This money is in the form of loans and grants for specific development projects and is in addition to the already mentioned $180 million in reparations. Dr. Adenauer's successors in office have been equally zealous in carrying out this commitment.

Apart from this, and by far the largest category of West German aid, is restitution to individual Israelis for suffering they or their families experienced under Hitler. These payments, wholly apart from the Adenauer-Sharett agreement, began in 1954 and now total well over $2 billion. Restitution of this kind will continue as long as the individual recipients are alive.

A second channel of indispensable aid to Israel is gifts and loans from individual Jews overseas, chiefly from American Jews, who number nearly 6 million—by far the largest Jewish community in the world. Consistently over the years American Jews have given at least $60 million annually to Israel through the United Jewish Appeal and another $50 million through the purchase of State of Israel bonds. These totals have swelled during crisis times, including the years since the 1967 war. Altogether, at least $5 billion has flowed into Israel from Jews overseas to help finance settlement, development, and defense costs.

If defense costs do not rise beyond their present level, Israeli officials hope to be able to stabilize the balance of payments deficit and even gradually reduce it. Israeli reserves of gold and foreign exchange, which had reached a high point of $750 million in 1967, dipped alarmingly to $380 million in 1969 because of the need to purchase arms abroad. The generosity of gifts from overseas has plugged this drain. Reserves at the beginning of 1971 stood at more than $400 million.

Israelis, then, depend on two continuing external factors —West German reparations and contributions from world Jewry.

(Communist East Germany, which claims that "capitalistic" West Germany is the "heir" of the Hitler regime, has given not one cent to Israel, and supports the Arabs unqualifiedly in their struggle with the Zionist state.) These two foreign channels, however, by no means relieve Israelis themselves of sacrifice, as attested to by the dramatic rises in domestic taxes in 1970.

"The real sacrifice," declared Dr. Eliezer Shefer, director of research for the Bank of Israel, "is in our standard of living, not in the development of the country."

With immigrants pouring in at an accelerated rate after the Six Day War, Israel's "infrastructure"—roads, communications, houses, schools, medical facilities—had to grow also. Otherwise the process of "ingathering" would have had to stop.

These settlement costs, plus defense needs, more than consumed whatever capital Israel was able to generate from abroad. "We were trying to do too much," said Dr. Shefer, "relative to the resources at our disposal. There was only one place to cut down."

That was in the area of private consumption. The hard work of Israelis was making the economy grow. In 1970 exports increased. So did the gross national product (GNP), the total of goods and services produced by the country. Yet, said Dr. Shefer, the people had to be told that they could not enjoy the fruits of their labor in a higher standard of living. Defense, development of the country, and settlement of newcomers had to come first.

This is why the government decreed higher taxes in 1970. The net effect was to drain off excess purchasing power, or, put another way, to reduce the amount of money individuals had left to spend on consumer goods.

Grumbling resulted, experts concede, particularly among Israelis at the lower end of the economic scale. The problem was complicated by the fact that many of these people were oriental Jews, some of whom read a discriminatory motive into what were actually purely economic measures. To help these people,

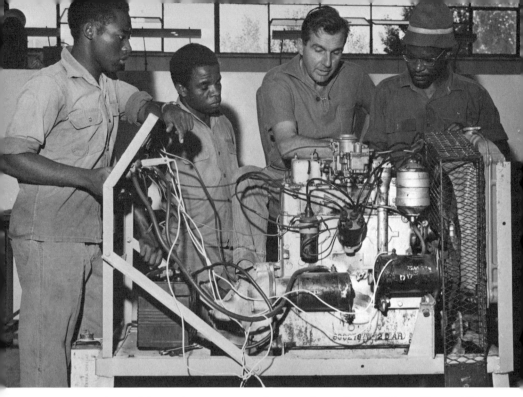

A machinery instructor teaches students from Africa. Many African lands send students to Israel to learn special skills.

and to deflate social pressures, the government paid compensation for price increases to families living below the poverty line.

Despite this dark picture, the Israeli economy has made substantial progress since the state was founded. The population of the country has more than trebled, which means that economic production has also had to treble, simply to keep the standard of living from declining. Israelis have done better than this. Their economy has expanded at an average annual rate of more than 9 percent, while the gross national product has grown 4.5 times since 1950.

The nation is rich in skilled people, poor in natural resources. The emphasis, therefore, is on producing finished products of high quality for export. Machinery, electrical and electronic components, cut diamonds, clothing, chemicals—these are staple exports, plus fresh and canned fruits and juices from the fertile coastal plain.

Israeli and West German merchants have set up three joint committees to facilitate the sale of Israeli products in Germany. One committee handles metal products, a second works with textiles and fashions, and the third markets fruits and vegetables. Jaffa orange and grapefruit juice, as well as other citrus products, are familiar items on German supermarket shelves.

The German who stops at his neighborhood florist to buy a bouquet for his wife or sweetheart may not realize that often he is buying flowers grown in Israel. Fresh roses, iris, gladioli, and other flowers are flown daily from the Jewish state to Germany.

The European Economic Community (EEC), or Common Market, poses a problem for Israel. Taken together, the six members of the EEC—West Germany, France, Italy, Belgium, Holland, and Luxembourg—buy nearly one-third of Israel's total exports. These products are subject to the common external tariff

Phosphate works near the Dead Sea.

erected by the EEC against imports from outside lands. The purpose of this measure is to give preference to domestic producers within the Common Market, whose goods flow back and forth throughout the community without tariffs.

Israel, to cut down this disparity, for years has sought an association agreement with the EEC similar to those enjoyed by Greece and Turkey. Such an agreement would progressively reduce the tariffs imposed by the EEC on Israeli goods. France, whose relations with the Jewish state soured during the regime of President Charles de Gaulle, has blocked full association for Israel. French-Israeli relations are slowly improving, but not yet to the extent of approving an association agreement for the Jewish state. Meanwhile, the six-nation EEC has agreed on a wide range of tariff concessions on Israeli goods, short of association. This agreement runs until 1975.

At one time France and Israel cooperated closely in matters of defense and atomic research. This occurred when France, embroiled in a war with Algeria, was regarded as an enemy by much of the Arab world. Then General de Gaulle gave independence to Algeria, and French-Arab relations, traditionally friendly in the past, grew warmer. De Gaulle's aim was to restore French influence among the Arabs, and for this reason his government reduced the visibility of its ties to Israel.

A climax came in 1967, when De Gaulle blamed Israel for starting the June war. The French government cut off the sale of new French weapons to Israel, including fifty Mirage V supersonic jet fighters, for which Israel had paid in full. Gradually French President Georges Pompidou, successor to General de Gaulle, is relaxing some aspects of this embargo on military sales to the Jewish state, and reportedly will repay to Israel the money spent for the blocked Mirages.

A key role in Israel's economy—indeed, in the nation's entire life—is played by Histadrut, or the General Federation of Labor. Americans are accustomed to powerful trade unions that

Visitors look at the Menorah, national symbol of Israel. The Knesset is in the background.

represent the interests of workers. But Histadrut sits on both sides of the bargaining table. It is Israel's largest employer, as well an all-embracing trade union organization.

This dual role sprang from Histadrut's function during the British mandate. Founded in 1920, when Jewish workers in Palestine numbered 5,000, Histadrut had to create jobs for incoming immigrants. There was no other agency to do this. The result was that the General Federation of Labor, through its ownership of enterprises, became employer as well as trade union. This duality persists, and today 90 percent of all Israeli workers are said to be affiliated in one way or another with Histadrut.

Two large construction firms—Solel Boneh and Koor, employing together about 40,000 workers—belong to Histadrut. The labor organization owns one of the three largest banks in Israel and publishes a morning newspaper called *Davar*. Ships, insurance companies, and various types of cooperative societies are operated by Histadrut. This "state within a state," as it has been called, markets products grown and manufactured by kibbutzim. Histadrut owns outright less than 30 percent of Israeli enterprises, though it shares ownership of some other factories and services with private business.

"We all belong to Histadrut," explained an Israeli official, "for a simple reason. We want health insurance."

During the mandate Histadrut organized health insurance and social welfare benefits for Jewish workers. In part this function, too, was carried over into statehood. Today Histadrut, not the government, operates the nation's comprehensive health insurance plan, though other elements of social welfare are handled by the government.

Histadrut owns 16 hospitals, more than 1,000 clinics, 16 rest homes, 260 pharmacies, and numerous other installations concerned with people's health. As a trade union organization—representing blue collar, white collar, and professional workers—and as the administrator of Israel's major health insurance plan, Histadrut directly touches the daily existence of most Israelis.

An economic factor of significance is Israel's growing stature as an oil producer. Before the Six Day War the Jewish state produced very little crude oil, buying most of its supplies from Iran. Israel still relies substantially on Iranian oil, which comes by tanker through the Strait of Tiran to the port of Eilat, where it is offloaded and pumped through a 42-inch pipeline across the Negev desert to Ashkelon on the Mediterranean coast. Here the oil is moved to refineries by ship and truck, and also through a smaller pipeline system to a refinery at Haifa.

Since 1967 Israel has been operating former Egyptian oil fields at Abu Rudeis in the Sinai Peninsula. These wells, which produce about 100,000 barrels daily, would be lost to Israel if the

Israeli army withdrew from Sinai as part of a peace agreement.

Early in 1971 Israel reported the discovery of oil in the Gulf of Suez, a narrow arm of water leading from the Red Sea to the southern terminus of the Suez Canal. On one side the Gulf of Suez is bordered by Egypt, on the other side by the Sinai Peninsula.

The future of Israeli wells in the Gulf of Suez depends on whether or not they lie in international waters. If the wells fall inside Egyptian territorial waters, presumably Israel will lose control of them in the event that it gives up Sinai. Retention of the wells, on the other hand, might mean that eventually Israel could reduce its balance of payments deficit through the sale of oil abroad.

9

Politics in Israel

Politically Israel is oriented toward socialism and the interests of the working class. This is not surprising, since Zionist ideology stressed the need for the scattered Jewish people to return to the soil and to primary pursuits. Many of the early Zionists who came to Palestine were deeply influenced by the doctrines of Karl Marx and other socialists.

As a result the political center of gravity in Israel, from 1948 to the present, has been located in the socialist parties, of which the largest is the Israel Labor Party. All of Israel's prime ministers, including Golda Meir, the present incumbent, have come from various factions of this party. So have Foreign Minister Abba Eban, Defense Minister Moshe Dayan, Deputy Premier Yigal Allon, and other cabinet ministers.

Israeli socialism requires careful definition. The nation's two small Communist parties, both of which are represented in the Knesset, stress Marxist ideology, as, to a lesser extent, does

Mapam, a democratic socialist party to the left of the Israel Labor Party.

But the latter, standing close to the center of the Israeli political spectrum, resembles the Social Democratic parties of Western Europe and the Labor Party of Britain. That is, the Israel Labor Party does not advocate nationalization of the nation's means of production, but supports the continued existence of free enterprise and of communal associations like the kibbutz. The Marxist flag, in other words, was hauled down long ago by Israel's major political party. This stance reflects the convictions of most Israelis.

Israel, though socialist in outlook, has a less comprehensive social welfare program than do such "capitalistic" nations as France and West Germany. Even in the United States, President Nixon, leader of a Republican Party dedicated to the concept of private enterprise, presented Congress with more far-reaching social welfare legislation than exists in Israel.

Unlike the United States, which has only two major political parties, Israel has a multiparty system. At the left are the two Communist factions (Maki and Rakah), then Mapam, and—broadly in the center—the Israel Labor Party. This party achieved its present name in 1968 through the merger of three socialist groups: Mapai, Achdut Ha'avoda-Poalei Zion, and Rafi.

To the right of the Israel Labor Party stands the Liberal Party, formed by the merger of the General Zionists and Progressives. These groups represent businessmen and some intellectuals, strongly in favor of free enterprise. Three religious parties exist, of which the strongest is the National Religious Party. The roles of religious groups in Israeli national life have already been discussed.

At the far right of the Israeli political spectrum is Herut, an outgrowth of the former terrorist organization Irgun Zvai Leumi. Menahem Begin, founder of Irgun, leads Herut. This militant party favors not only the retention of most Arab lands now held by Israel, but the eventual expansion of the Jewish state to its historical biblical boundaries, as they were under King David and his son Solomon. Such enlargement would, among other things, push Israel east of the Jordan River, obliterating King Hussein's Jordanian realm. Herut commands only minority support among Israelis. Within the Knesset, Herut and the Liberal Party form an alliance called Gahal.

Apart from the parties listed above, several splinter groups exist, expressing diverse points of view.

Supreme legislative authority in Israel is vested in the 120-seat, one-chamber Knesset, which is elected by universal suffrage for a term of four years. Citizens do not cast their votes for individuals, as in the United States, but for party lists. This system, known as proportional representation, means that if a party wins 30 percent of the national vote it gets 30 percent of the Knesset seats, and so on down the line.

The Knesset, as the collective voice of the people, can overrule the Supreme Court, as was illustrated by the historic "who is a Jew" controversy. The Israeli Supreme Court, unlike its counterpart in the United States, cannot invalidate laws passed by the Knesset.

Executive power—authority to conduct the nation's affairs, at home and abroad—belongs to the cabinet, or government, headed by the prime minister. The government, as in Britain and many western European countries, is responsible to parliament. The latter can turn the government out of office through a vote of no confidence. This differs from the American system, under which a president remains in office for four years whether or not his party has a majority in Congress.

The Knesset elects the president of Israel for a term of five years. His functions are largely ceremonial. As chief of state the president receives the credentials of foreign ambassadors and

An Arab deputy speaks in the Knesset.

signs laws and treaties after their ratification. When a new government is to be formed, the president consults the parties and formally asks the appropriate party leader to form a cabinet.

The president gives his nod of approval not to his own favorite, but to that individual chosen by the party or coalition which commands a majority in the Knesset. This is essentially the same role as that played by the queen in England or the president of the German Federal Republic. Israel's parliamentary democracy, in short, is modeled on European lines, reflecting the fact that most of the Jewish state's founding fathers came from Europe.

A word should be said about a special category of Israelis —the approximately 320,000 Arabs who are citizens of the Jewish state. These people include Arabs who did not flee in 1948, their children, and the nearly 100,000 Palestine Arabs who have been allowed to return to their homes under family reunion plans. These 320,000 Arab citizens lived in Israel before 1967 and are distinguished from the 70,000 Arabs of Old Jerusalem, who came under Israeli control only after the Six Day War.

The Arabs of Jerusalem, to whom the Israeli government gave the status of "permanent residents" in 1967, can vote only in Jerusalem municipal elections. Israel's original Arab citizens enjoy fuller rights. They can, and do, send their own representatives to the Knesset. Arab deputies are allowed to speak Arabic from the rostrum of parliament, though Hebrew is the nation's dominant language.

A number of Arabs vote Communist, though they may not personally be Marxists. The Rakah faction of the Communists, with three deputies in the current Knesset, toes the Moscow line and demands the withdrawal of Israeli forces from occupied Arab lands. By casting votes for Rakah, many Israeli Arabs see a way to demonstrate legally their opposition to the Jewish state. Two of Rakah's three Knesset deputies are Arabs. Mapam, the left-wing socialist party, also welcomes Arab members and strives to create conditions of equality for all citizens of the country.

In one limited area Arab Israelis possess rights beyond those granted to Jews. Rabbinical courts, we recall, handle matters of marriage and divorce for Jewish Israelis. "Moslems, however," declared a Jewish legal expert, "go to their own religious courts in Israel for *all* matters of personal status—not only marriage and divorce, but also for problems of inheritance, adjudication of wills, and so on."

The Israeli government has spent much money to modernize the villages of its Arab citizens. Water and electricity have been brought to rural areas; irrigation networks have been established. Arab farmers have been taught advanced methods of agriculture. More than half of all Arab workers belong to Histadrut, which safeguards their professional and social rights as it does those of its Jewish members.

Efforts are being made to uplift nomadic Bedouin Arabs by settling them on the land. On the rocky slopes between Beer-sheba and the Dead Sea, in the northern Negev, I saw school buildings put up by the Israeli government for the children of tent-dwelling Bedouins. Each morning Bedouin children leave the goat-hair tents of their families, pitched in the valleys near the schools, and trek by foot, donkey, or camel off to class.

There is little reason to doubt Jewish sincerity in these efforts to help Arab citizens. For Israelis to host a large and permanently hostile minority is, after all, of no benefit to them. But there is a point beyond which neither side can go, given the general situation of Arab-Jewish confrontation in the Middle East.

Israeli Arabs except for the Druze do not have the right— or the obligation, depending on the point of view—to serve in the Israeli army. A few have been accepted as volunteers, after care-

Arabs come to trade at the Bedouin market in Beersheba. (Israel Government Tourist Office)

*Bedouin woman
and child.
(A. Berger)*

ful scrutiny of their backgrounds. But the loyalty of many Israeli
Arabs is assumed by the Jews to lie with the Arab side. Others,
with relatives living in Arab countries, might be subject to black
mail.

Admittedly this poses a dilemma for Israel. The government strives to convince its Arabs that they are equal citizens
with Jews. Yet the Jewish majority withholds full trust, by refusing to accept Arab young men as soldiers. This causes bitterness
among those Arabs—and there are some—who, for better or
worse, have cast their lot with the Jewish state.

For years after 1948 Israeli Arabs were kept under military surveillance. They could move from one area to another

Two Druze from Galilee. Their minority status in Israel was recently abolished. (Israel Government Tourist Office)

only with special permission. Gradually these restrictions were eased, until, on December 1, 1966, they were abolished. Today Arab citizens of Israel travel freely throughout the country.

A minority of Arab Israelis are Druze, members of a religious sect which broke away from the main body of Islam centuries ago. Since that break Druze minorities have lived a sometimes tense existence in Arab lands, notably Syria, Lebanon, and Palestine. Hostility between the Druze and orthodox Moslems has led to an apparent identification of interests between Jewish Israelis and the Druze living in the Zionist state. Druze men are drafted into the army and are regarded by the Jews as tough and reliable soldiers.

Until 1970 the Israeli Druze were classified as a special minority group along with Moslem Arabs, Christians, Circassians, and Samaritans. Government relations with minority groups are administered by a section of the premier's office. Druze leaders, arguing that the proven loyalty of their soldiers was shared by all 33,300 members of the Druze community, urged the government to abolish the minority status for Israeli Druze. The government did so and the Druze moved a step closer toward full assimilation in the society of Israel.

As a class, Israeli Arabs are economically better off than their brethren on the West Bank or in Jordan. Yet the natural desire of most of them, presumably, is to be governed by Arabs, not Jews. Also, Arab citizens of Israel cannot be certain how the chips of peace may fall. In their hearts many do not foreclose the possibility of living again in an Arab state. Meanwhile, they are fully aware that undue cooperation with Israel might be considered by outside Arabs to be collaboration with the enemy.

Among a group of Israelis I met a pretty dark-haired young woman in her early twenties. In dress and appearance she was indistinguishable from a Jew. But she was an Arab—a schoolteacher of Arab children. "Who else is going to teach our children about their heritage and culture?" she demanded. "Should they learn about it from Jews?"

Her motive was to help her people. Yet many Arabs, particularly the fierce commandos who live and operate in Jordan, might regard this girl as a traitor because she was, in effect, a civil servant of Israel.

Under such circumstances only lasting peace in the Middle East can bring real equality to the more than 300,000 Arabs who, whether they like it or not, now live in a Jewish state.

The Soviet Union, to further its own ends in the Middle East, has done much to fan Arab hatred of Israel. Russian efforts to penetrate the area date back to the czars, who sought warm-water access—either the Persian Gulf, or the Mediterranean Sea, or both—for the ships of their vast northern realm. These efforts at penetration, which were continued by the Bolshevik successors to the czars, were frustrated by western powers, principally Britain and France.

After World War II the Soviet leaders at first befriended Israel, hoping to use the Jewish state as an instrument to promote Russian goals. Thus the Soviet Union secretly supplied weapons to the Jewish Haganah in Palestine. In 1947 Moscow supported the UN partition plan and even criticized the Arabs for opposing it. Soviet recognition of the State of Israel in May 1948 was swift.

A turning point in Soviet policy came in 1953, when a bomb thrown at the Soviet Embassy in Tel Aviv led Moscow to break diplomatic relations with Israel. This coincided with a wave of anti-Semitism in Russia during the last years of Stalin's life. The Soviet leaders who succeeded Stalin also concluded that President Nasser of Egypt, whose star was rising rapidly throughout the Arab world, should be cultivated by Moscow. The Kremlin now decided to back the Arabs against Israel.

Moscow's opportunity came in 1955 when the United States refused to sell arms to Cairo, and President Nasser turned to the Soviets for weapons. Quickly the Soviet Union agreed to supply Egypt with modern weapons, to be paid for by future shipments of Egyptian cotton. A similar, though smaller, arms deal was signed with Syria.

The Soviets also agreed to finance a number of technical aid projects in both sectors of the United Arab Republic, when Egypt and Syria briefly merged their countries. The supply of Soviet weapons later was extended to Iraq and, to a lesser extent, to Algeria. Today the Egyptian, Syrian, and Iraqi armies are almost totally dependent on the Soviet Union for military supplies.

Egypt, more than any other Arab country, has become the focus of Soviet penetration of the Middle East. President Nasser, striving to enlarge his influence throughout the Arab world, posed himself as the chief Arab opponent of Israel. To substantiate this role, Nasser needed more and more military equipment from the Soviets and eventually accepted thousands of Russian advisers in his country.

Israeli soldiers maintain a watch at the east bank of the Suez Canal. (*Israel Sun*)

Egypt, from Moscow's point of view, is ideally located at the crossroads of Asia and Africa. Geographically the UAR can serve the Soviets as a potential springboard into Africa. The Suez Canal, which cuts through Egyptian territory, can be used by the Soviets to establish a link between their growing naval fleets in the Indian Ocean and the Mediterranean Sea. Moscow has shown great interest in having the canal reopened, as part of a peace settlement between Israel and the Arabs.

President Nasser drew a line between his friendship for the Soviet Union and his hostility to the Egyptian Communist Party, which is outlawed in Egypt. Nasser's policy in this regard has been followed by President Sadat. The Kremlin soon showed it was willing to jettison its support of Egyptian Communists in favor of closer ties with Mr. Nasser and now President Sadat. The welfare of Egyptian Communists, in other words, takes second place to Moscow's larger interests in the Middle East.

In July 1971 the USSR protested sharply to the Sudan, Egypt's southern neighbor, when the Sudanese government began executing a number of Sudanese Communists. The Communists had been implicated in a leftist coup to overthrow the Sudanese regime led by President Gaafar al-Nimeiry. When General Nimeiry regained power, his government tried and executed leaders of the plot. Moscow warned President Nimeiry that he was jeopardizing future deliveries of Soviet economic and military aid, which had begun to flow to Khartoum, Sudan's capital, in 1969.

The Kremlin's tactics in this respect vary from country to country. In some Arab countries the Soviet Union works partly through local Communists to promote its interests. In Egypt, however, where Soviet influence in the Middle East is centered, the Russians emphasize their relations with President Sadat and virtually ignore his ban on political activities by the Communist Party.

The Soviets made a deliberate decision to rearm Egyptian forces after the Six Day War, during which the UAR army and air force lost the bulk of its Soviet equipment in Sinai. Apparently, however, as part of the price of acquiring new weapons, the Egyptians agreed to—or were forced to—accept more Soviet military advisers. Western experts now place the number of Soviet military personnel in Egypt at about 10,000, including hundreds of generals and admirals. This is considered to be far more than Egypt would need for training purposes.

Almost all major items of equipment, including jet fighters and bombers, tanks, artillery pieces, and various types of rockets, have been supplied to the UAR by the Soviets since 1967. Much of this equipment is of the most modern type, including SAM-3 (surface-to-air) missiles. These missiles ring major Egyptian cities and also are clustered along the west side of the Suez Canal. Beyond this, the Soviets have greatly increased the number of ships in their Mediterranean fleet.

Consistently the Soviets have tried to avoid a direct confrontation with the United States in the Middle East which might lead to war. With this concern in mind, the Soviets do not appear to want a new round of Arab-Israeli fighting, at least at this point. Soviet newspapers have warned Arab commandos against trying to recapture Palestine by force. Moscow's public policy is committed to finding a political settlement between Arabs and Israelis. Nonetheless, the Soviets continue to arm the Arabs and to support them diplomatically, in the UN and elsewhere, against Israel.

In varying degree a Soviet military, economic, and political presence is found today in the UAR, Syria, Iraq, Algeria, the Sudan, Yemen, and South Yemen. At the end of World War II Soviet influence in the Arab world was almost nonexistent.

A high water mark of Soviet-Egyptian cooperation came on May 27, 1971, when President Nikolai Podgorny and President Sadat signed in Cairo a fifteen-year Treaty of Friendship and Cooperation. Pledging "unbreakable friendship" between the two countries, the treaty calls for the "exchange of experience in the economic, scientific, and technological fields—in industry, agriculture, water conservancy, irrigation, the development of power engineering, the training of national personnel and other fields of the economy." Cooperation in the arts, the press, radio, television, tourism, and the cinema also is prescribed.

Article 8 of the treaty forecasts continued Soviet military aid to the UAR. "Such cooperation," the treaty reads, "will provide specifically for assistance in the training of UAR military personnel and in mastering the armaments and equipment supplied to the United Arab Republic with a view to strengthening its capacity to eliminate the consequences of the aggression as well as increasing its ability to stand up to aggression in general."

The "consequences of the aggression" referred to means Israel's occupation of the Gaza Strip and the Sinai Peninsula.

We recall that Moscow broke diplomatic relations with Israel in 1953. These relations later were restored, only to be severed again because of the 1956 Sinai war. The Soviets, however, apparently valued the opportunity to talk directly with Israeli officials and once again opened their embassy in Tel Aviv. A third break, which still exists, came in June 1967. In mid-1971 the Soviet government began to make overtures about reestablishing diplomatic relations with Israel.

The Soviet Union, with nearly 2.5 million Jewish citizens, has more Jews than any other country except the United States and Israel itself. Many Soviet Jews, though not all, want to emigrate to the Zionist state. Soviet officials have been reluctant to let them go, partly because a mass departure would speak ill of life under communism and Soviet rule.

In 1969 about 2,000 Soviet Jews were allowed to leave the country. The following year the total dropped to approximately 1,000. In 1971 the Soviet government partially liberalized emigration procedures, and 13,000 Jews were allowed to leave. This action followed worldwide protests over trials of Soviet Jews in Leningrad on charges of anti-Soviet activity of various kinds.

By permitting more Jews to emigrate, Soviet authorities may have hoped to defuse criticism of the trials. There is no indication, however, that Kremlin policy has basically changed, though Israeli officials hope as many as 30,000 Soviet Jews may be allowed to emigrate in 1972.

10

The United States and Israel

After World War I, when President Wilson sent a fact-finding mission to the Middle East, the United States was the most popular western power among the Arabs. Colonial rivalry between France and Britain had colored Arab views on those two states. America had no colonial ambitions in the Middle East.

The American presence in the Arab world was of a different sort—made up primarily of Protestant missionary educators who, beginning in the nineteenth century, had gone to Lebanon, Palestine, Syria, and Egypt to found schools and medical missions. Thousands of Arab youngsters passed through these schools over the years, learning English and shaping their vision of America largely from the teachers to whom they were exposed.

Many of these Arab students went on to the American University of Beirut, perched high on a hill above the Mediterranean Sea, or to the American University of Cairo. Some Arab

leaders to whom President Wilson's envoys talked were gradu-
ates of these institutions. It was against this background that
Arabs above all opted for an American mandate, if they had to
endure one at all.

Today, approximately fifty years later, the United States is
widely unpopular throughout the Arab world. Seven Arab countries, led by Egypt, have no diplomatic relations with Washington. These states, charging the United States government with
bias toward Israel, broke relations after the June 1967 war.

What has happened, in the last fifty-odd years, to drain so
nearly dry the once-brimming reservoir of Arab goodwill toward
America? The answer lies in the progressive involvement of the
United States in the Arab-Jewish conflict since World War II.

Colonel William A. Eddy, United States Minister to Saudi
Arabia from 1944 to 1946, described after his retirement how he
and three other American diplomats serving in the Arab world
were recalled to Washington in 1946 by President Harry S. Truman. They were asked by the president to analyze Arab reaction
to American policy in Palestine. The diplomats replied that one-
sided support of the Zionist cause would jeopardize American relations with the Arabs.

"Mr. Truman," wrote Colonel Eddy, "summed up his position with the utmost candor: 'I'm sorry, gentlemen, but I have to
answer to hundreds of thousands who are anxious for the success
of Zionism: I do not have hundreds of thousands of Arabs among
my constituents.'" [1]

President Truman meant that the great majority of American Jews, anguished by the Nazi holocaust just ended in Europe,
were pressing the United States government to support the establishment of a Jewish state in Palestine. Many American Christians, horrified by what had happened to European Jewry, felt

---

[1] William A. Eddy, *F.D.R. Meets Ibn Saud* (New York: American Friends of
the Middle East, Inc., 1954), pp. 36–37.

the same way. Humanitarianism did much to shape American policy toward Israel.

But a visible thread of domestic politics ran through the whole affair. Democratic and Republican politicians, running for office in cities and states with large Jewish constituencies, vied to outdo each other in expressing commitment to the Zionist cause. Very few raised the question of what was happening to American interests in the Arab world, although American oil companies already were investing millions of dollars in Arab lands.

In 1947, as we have noted, the United Nations voted to partition Palestine into a Jewish and an Arab state. A straw vote taken before the actual balloting indicated that the necessary two-thirds majority for partition could not be mustered. American Zionist leaders, including nationally known figures in public life, urged six small nations, who were opposed to partition, to change their vote. Several of these states were deeply dependent on American economic aid. In the end four of the target countries—Haiti, Liberia, Ethiopia, and the Philippines—reversed their stand and voted for partition. Of the other two, Nationalist China abstained and Greece stuck to its guns and voted against the resolution.

The United States, we recall, was the first foreign power to recognize the State of Israel when it was proclaimed on May 14, 1948. Washington's next step was to support the infant Jewish state with substantial economic help, which, until the late 1050s, far outweighed the amount of aid the United States gave to *all* Arab states combined. In the first twelve years of Israel's existence, the United States furnished $614,300,000 in various forms of aid to the Jewish state, compared with $386,480,000 to all Arab countries. This official help was apart from the hundreds of millions of dollars which American Jewish citizens poured privately into Israel during the same period.

Having done so much to bring Israel into existence, the

United States was honor-bound to help the Zionist state through its formative years. But Arab governments and peoples had a different point of view. The creation of Israel, as the Arabs saw it, had robbed the Arabs of Palestine and put to flight nearly one million Palestinians, who became a charge on surrounding Arab lands.

All this, the Arabs reasoned, had been made possible by big-power support, primarily that of the United States. When the United States, Britain, and France concluded the Tripartite Declaration of 1950, guaranteeing the territorial integrity of Middle Eastern states, the Arabs construed this as putting a seal of approval on Israel's wartime expansion beyond the 1947 partition lines.

Meanwhile, American commercial and strategic interests in the Arab world were growing. The United States itself did not depend greatly on Arab oil. But western Europe and Japan drew their petroleum supplies primarily from Arab sources. American companies, particularly in Saudi Arabia and Kuwait, controlled a major part of this production. Beyond this, the loss of Arab oil to

Oil pipelines. American oil companies have invested millions of dollars in Arab lands. (Standard Oil Company, New Jersey)

western Europe and to Japan would have forced the United States to deplete its own domestic reserves to keep its allies supplied.

This was one reason the United States government was deeply concerned to minimize Soviet influence in the Middle East. Strategy was another factor. Communist control of the Middle East would have cut western defense links with southern Asia and the Far East. All this, American diplomats reasoned, dictated a policy of friendship toward the Arabs. Yet the possibilities of friendship were undercut by Washington's political and economic bias toward Israel.

Open partiality to Israel ended when President Eisenhower succeeded Mr. Truman in office. President Eisenhower did not cut back on American support of the Jewish state. But he sought to strike a balance by increasing American technical, economic, and financial aid to Arab governments. He also put decisive pressure on Israel to withdraw from Sinai after the second Arab-Israeli war in 1956.

Ironically, Soviet influence among the Arabs mushroomed during General Eisenhower's term of office. In 1955 President Nasser appealed to the United States to sell Egypt military equipment. Morale among the Egyptian officer corps, Nasser explained, was low, particularly following an Israeli army raid in Gaza in February 1955, during which thirty-eight Egyptian soldiers were killed. Nasser needed new weapons, he told Washington, not to use offensively against Israel, but to improve the morale of his army.

Secretary of State John Foster Dulles, backed up by President Eisenhower, refused to sell Egypt arms. This Cairo-Washington dialogue took place against the backdrop of the newly formed Baghdad Pact, an alliance of pro-western states in the Middle East sponsored by Britain and the United States. The idea had been to erect an anti-Communist bulwark, designed to screen out Soviet encroachment from the north.

From the standpoint of Arab-American relations, however, the Baghdad Pact boomeranged. Iraq was the only Arab state to join, the other members being Turkey, Iran, and Pakistan. President Nasser viewed the pact as an attack on his concept of "positive neutrality" among the Arabs in the East-West dispute. He also interpreted the alliance as an Anglo-American effort to strengthen anti-Nasser elements in Iraq and other Arab lands.

Mr. Dulles, for his part, was convinced that Nasser was trying to overthrow pro-western governments in the Arab world. In this atmosphere of mutual distrust the projected arms deal fell through. Nasser's response was to accept a Soviet offer of weapons.

Nasser now had become, in Mr. Dulles' eyes, the villain who had opened the Middle East to the Soviet Union. The American reaction was to punish Egypt by barring the sale of lubricating oils to Cairo, ending a CARE school lunch program for Egyptian children, and otherwise bringing economic pressure to bear. Dulles also withdrew an American offer to help Egypt build the Aswan High Dam. Moscow stepped in here, too, with the result that the Soviet Union gained credit for constructing a project on which Egypt's economic future largely depends.

Nasser's next move was to nationalize the Suez Canal, which led to the French-British-Israeli invasion of Egypt in 1956. President Eisenhower's insistence that the three invading powers withdraw their troops was welcomed by the Arabs. But this could not offset the damage already done to Arab-American relations, first by the Truman administration's partiality to Israel and then by the Dulles-Nasser contretemps.

American policy toward the Middle East entered a third phase under Presidents John F. Kennedy and Lyndon B. Johnson. One strand of this policy was based on recognition that Nasser, whether Washington liked it or not, was the dominant Arab leader. The United States would be courting trouble throughout the Arab world if it ignored Nasser or tried to work against him.

President Nasser of Egypt addressing the General Assembly of the United Nations in 1960. (United Nations)

Egypt's overwhelming social problems, springing from the country's runaway population growth, seemed to be a fruitful area for potential American-Egyptian cooperation. In 1963 President Kennedy's administration gave Egypt $220 million worth of help, mainly in foodstuffs. Israel that same year received $80 million in American aid.

A second strand of American policy called for support of King Hussein of Jordan, who was increasingly challenged by militant Palestinians living in his realm. Hussein had shown himself to be a moderate, western-oriented Arab leader, whose disappearance would have undermined stability in the Middle East. American economic aid, plus the sale of selected military equipment to Jordan, were designed to help the king keep his country under control. American oil investments in Saudi Arabia and the Persian Gulf sheikdoms, now worth billions of dollars, also were to be safeguarded by maintaining as good relations as possible with the governments of the oil-producing states.

King Hussein of Jordan.
(*United Nations*)

None of this, as the United States government saw it, weakened traditional American support of Israel. Israeli leaders were not so sure. They argued that increased American aid to Cairo released Egyptian resources for the purchase of additional Soviet arms. In 1963 Prime Minister Ben-Gurion of Israel claimed to have indisputable evidence that the Arabs were planning to attack the Jewish state. He demanded a Soviet-American guarantee of Israel's frontiers. Failing that, the Israeli leader wanted a mutual defense pact between Israel and the United States.

He obtained neither one. The Soviet purpose in the Middle East was not to reduce tension, but to use the Arab-Israel dispute to extend Moscow's influence in the Arab world.

President Kennedy, for his part, refused to negotiate an Israeli-American mutual defense pact. Such an arrangement automatically would have committed the United States to go to Israel's defense should it be attacked. Neither Kennedy nor any later American president was prepared to go that far.

President Kennedy did, however, quietly insure—through the sale of aircraft and other weapons systems to Israel—that a rough Arab-Israeli military balance was maintained. This policy has been continued to the present. Each significant accretion of Soviet weapons by Egypt is matched by a flow of American arms to Israel.

By the spring of 1967 three American presidents— Eisenhower, Kennedy, and Johnson—had fostered the concept of American neutrality between Arabs and Jews. This policy was based on the conviction that Arab nationalism not only must be lived with, but that it also provides a barrier against the growth of domestic communism in Arab lands.

As 1967 wore on, the likelihood of another Arab-Jewish clash grew increasingly evident. On May 23, 1967, two weeks before the third round of fighting broke out, President Johnson defined American policy as follows:

> To the leaders of all the nations of the Near East, I wish to say what American Presidents have said before me—that the United States is firmly committed to the support of the political independence and territorial integrity of all nations of that area. The United States strongly opposes aggression by anyone in the area in any form, overt or clandestine.

Israel's lightning victory in June 1967, during which its army seized territory from Syria, Jordan, and Egypt, placed the United States in an awkward position. According to Mr. Johnson's formula, Washington was bound to press the Israelis to give up their conquered lands. On June 13, a week after the Israeli army had rewritten the Middle Eastern map, Mr. Johnson indicated that the United States would urge Israel to do just that. "That is our policy," the president declared, referring to his earlier statement of May 23. "It will continue to be our policy."

The "territorial integrity of all nations," in other words, to which the United States was "firmly committed," covered Arab states as well as Israel.

The Security Council of the United Nations, on November 22, 1967, passed a resolution to which the United States government subscribed. This resolution, designed to bring about "a just and lasting peace" in the Middle East, called for concessions from both sides to the Arab-Israel dispute. Key points of the November 22, 1967, resolution, on which current peace-seeking efforts are based, are as follows:

1. Israel was urged to withdraw from all Arab territory occupied during the 1967 fighting.

2. The "sovereignty, territorial integrity, and political independence of every State in the area" should be recognized. All states of belligerency were to cease. (The Arabs, in other words, were being asked to acknowledge the right of the State of Israel to exist as a recognized political entity and to agree to live in peace with their Jewish neighbor.)

3. All Middle Eastern states had the "right to live in peace within secure and recognized boundaries free from threats or acts of force." (This implied the replacement of the 1948 "armistice" lines and the 1967 "ceasefire" borders with permanent frontiers.)

4. International waterways were to be open to ships of all nations.

5. Secretary General U Thant was requested to send a special representative to the Middle East, to act as a go-between to lead the two sides to a peace agreement. U Thant named Gunnar Jarring, Swedish ambassador to Moscow, as his special envoy.

Perhaps the most disputed element of the UN resolution involves the phrase "secure and recognized boundaries." Should this mean, as the Arabs insist, a withdrawal by Israel to pre-1967 frontiers? The language of the November 22 resolution is unequivocal. Israeli armed forces are called upon to renounce their gains.

The Israeli government refuses, claiming that only "defensible" frontiers qualify as "secure" boundaries. Defensible, from the Israeli point of view, means borders that can be defended against Arab attack by Israeli forces alone.

This brings Israel into conflict with American policy. President Nixon and Secretary of State William P. Rogers urge Israel to put its trust in frontiers guaranteed by the United Nations, including the United States. Israel should withdraw from the occupied territories, according to the American idea. A UN peacekeeping force, including American, Soviet, British, French, and perhaps other foreign troops, would then step between the Arabs and Israelis along the sensitive frontiers. The UN should stipulate, in the American view, that no single power could cause this peacekeeping force to be withdrawn, as happened in 1967, when

UN military observers on duty in the Suez Canal sector. (United Nations)

President Nasser ordered the blue helmets out of Gaza and Sharm el-Sheikh.

Israeli officials, including Prime Minister Golda Meir, remain skeptical. They note, first of all, that the United States offers no unilateral guarantee of Israel's future borders, but only an American presence within an international force. Second, Israelis foresee the possibility that some future Egyptian, or other Arab, government might regard itself as not bound by the United Nations arrangement. The only way to bind the Arabs, in the Israeli view, is to have them sit down with the Israelis and negotiate a peace treaty. As part of such face-to-face discussions, but not before, Israel would be willing to consider giving up some of the occupied lands, though not all.

Having evolved through the Truman, Eisenhower, and later phases, current United States policy toward Israel includes the following major elements:

Washington is unwilling to grant Israel a defense guarantee, such as the United States extends to its NATO allies. The North Atlantic Treaty of 1949 holds that an armed attack against one or more NATO members is an attack against them all. Thus Luxembourg, or Belgium, or Iceland, is sheltered beneath an American defense umbrella, which Israel cannot share.

The Tripartite Declaration of 1950, whereby the United States, Britain, and France undertook to guarantee Arab-Israel borders, is not the kind of commitment the Israelis want from Washington. This three-power agreement protects Arabs as much as Israelis and, if taken at face value, requires the United States to seek Israeli withdrawal from Arab-occupied lands.

The United States has agreed to supply the Jewish state with whatever weapons are needed to prevent the Arabs from achieving a military advantage.

Israeli shipping should have unrestricted access to all international waterways in the area, including the Suez Canal and the Strait of Tiran.

Secretary Rogers, during a trip to the Middle East in 1971, urged Israeli and Egyptian leaders to consider a bilateral agreement to reopen the Suez Canal. This agreement, which would be separate from overall Arab-Israeli negotiations, would provide for a partial pullback of Israeli forces in Sinai and a commitment by the UAR not to reoccupy the east bank of the canal. The waterway then could be cleared and put back to work for all nations of the world.

President Sadat insists on the right of Egyptian troops to cross the canal, on the grounds that the Sinai Peninsula belongs to the UAR. Israel refuses, under these conditions, to give up its positions along the east bank. As a consequence, no agreement on opening the canal has been achieved.

Arab governments should accept the legitimacy of Israel and its right to live in peace as an independent state.

Beyond all this, an implicit assumption exists that the United States never would stand by and let Israel be destroyed by any combination of hostile forces. This, of course, falls short of the formal guarantee which Israel wants.

Such is the policy of the United States government, based on official neutrality between Arabs and Israelis. The administration in Washington is under steady political pressure from domestic Zionist forces to adopt a more pro-Israeli course. An example of this was a paid advertisement, signed by 59 United States senators and 238 representatives, which appeared in a number of American newspapers in the spring of 1969.

This ad, placed by the American Israel Public Affairs Committee, Inc., was headlined: "A Declaration . . . in favor of Direct Arab-Israel Peace Negotiations, on the occasion of Israel's 21st birthday, April 23rd, 1969, Endorsed by a majority of the Senate and House of Representatives."

The declaration began by congratulating Israel on two decades of progress. The lawmakers then expressed "concern that the people of Israel are still denied their right to peace and that they must carry heavy defense burdens which divert human and material resources from productive pursuits."

> We deeply regret [the statement continued] that Israel's Arab neighbors, after three futile and costly wars, still refuse to negotiate a final peace settlement with Israel. We believe that the issues which divide Israel and the Arab states can be resolved . . . if the leaders of the Arab states would agree to meet with Israelis in face-to-face negotiations. . . . We oppose any attempt by outside powers to impose halfway measures not conducive to a permanent peace.

This last sentence is significant. At the moment the advertisement appeared, President Nixon was engaged in seeking a Big Four solution to the Middle East impasse with the Soviet Union, Britain, and France. Mr. Nixon's intention was not to impose a settlement on Arabs and Jews. But he felt that if the Big Four could agree on the outline of a reasonable settlement, United Nations representatives might persuade Arabs and Israelis to fill in the details. A State Department official described the Big Four talks as a "catalyst," designed to create a "substantive framework in which parties directly concerned can develop their dialogue."

Israel opposed this approach on the grounds that Arab governments later might repudiate an agreement worked out by the Big Four. More than half the elected representatives of the American people were saying, in effect, that they disagreed with United States government policy and agreed with Israel. Signing the advertisement were Republicans and Democrats, both conservative and liberal. Such a mixed bag of American legislators probably could not be brought to take issue with their own government's policy on any other foreign problem.

In other ways the Arab-Israel dispute has intruded into domestic American affairs. On December 18, 1957, the American tanker *National Peace*, under contract to the United States navy, was refused port facilities to pick up an oil cargo at Ras Tannura, Saudi Arabia. The Saudis took the action because, under the name S. S. *Memory*, the tanker earlier had traded with Israel. The navy canceled its contract with the *National Peace* and chose another vessel. Owners of the *National Peace* then sued the navy for breach of contract and damages of $160,000.

The navy, to prevent a repetition, introduced the so-called Haifa clause into its oil-tanker contracts. This clause gave the navy the right to cancel its charter if the ship in question were denied entry into an Arab port because of previous trade with Israel. The Haifa clause appeared to rule out competition for contracts by American ships which had done business in Israeli ports.

Challenged by Congress to explain its decision, the navy insisted it was not bowing to the Arab League economic boycott of Israel. Rather, U.S. navy officials were trying to prevent needless expense to American taxpayers. Nonetheless, congressional pressure caused the navy to agree in 1960 to eliminate the Haifa clause from future contracts.

A similar issue arose in 1960, when the American Jewish Congress charged the U.S. Department of Agriculture and the Commodity Credit Corporation with refusal to ship United States government foodstuffs to Egypt on ships which had traded with Israel. The goods involved were cargoes of surplus farm products sold under the Public Law 480 program. American officials stressed that taxpayers' money would be wasted if a ship which had traded with Israel were loaded with wheat and sent to Alexandria or some other Arab port only to be turned away.

On April 13, 1960, the Seafarers International Union threw a picket line around the Egyptian ship *Cleopatra* in New York harbor. American stevedores of the International Longshoremen's Association refused to unload her cargo. Paul Hall, head of the SIU, denied that Zionist pressure was involved. He said the action had been taken to protest the loss of American seamen's jobs because of the Arab economic boycott of Israel. Some American shipowners, according to Mr. Hall, were refusing to trade with Israel lest their vessels be blacklisted by the Arabs.

Arab trade union leaders, describing the *Cleopatra* incident as a "Zionist-imperialist plot," ordered American ships to be boycotted in all Arab ports, from Morocco to Iraq. This Arab boycott was completely effective. American ships could not be unloaded in Arab ports, even though their cargoes included emergency wheat shipments destined for hungry Syrians, suffering from a third straight year of drought.

The State Department agreed to seek an end to the blacklisting of American ships by the economic boycott office of the Arab League. The SIU then withdrew its pickets from the *Cleopatra* and business returned to normal. In fact, there was little the State Department could do, except hope that such incidents would not arise again.

For years the U.S. air force was unable to send American Jewish servicemen to its giant air base at Dhahran, Saudi Arabia, because the Saudis refused to grant visas to Jews of any nationality. Since the Dhahran base was considered important to American security, the United States was forced to assign air force personnel who could obtain Saudi visas. The State Department, accused by the American Jewish Congress of submitting to foreign discrimination against American citizens, replied that it was making every effort to have the practice ended. This particular problem became academic when the Dhahran base was deactivated.

After the 1967 Middle Eastern war, seven Arab governments, we recall, broke diplomatic relations with the United States. Some Arab governments took other retaliatory measures against American interests, including temporary oil embargoes, the closing of certain cultural institutions, and the sequestration of property. Both the American University of Cairo and the American University of Beirut were allowed to remain open. Arab leaders, however unhappy they might be with United

States policy, recognized the educational value to their own peoples of these two institutions.

Given the fact that nearly 6 million Americans are Jews, many of them influential in political, financial, and other spheres; and given the fact that Israel's viability depends ultimately on the continuing generosity of American Jews—all this, plus the natural sympathy of Americans for a people which has suffered much, means that United States relations with the Jewish state are bound to remain both close and controversial.

11

The Morality of the Case

The scene was the *majlis*, or council room, of the sheik of a small Arab town on the West Bank of the Jordan River. The room was plain, with wooden chairs ranged around the walls and a kerosene stove bubbling away in the center, giving warmth to the men clustered in the room. They were all Arabs, a few wearing western suits but most of them in flowing robes, with headcloths wound around their heads. Their leader was an elderly, portly Arab, the sheik, or mayor of the town.

A car approached outside, and a stir of anticipation ran through the group. The door opened, and into the majlis strode three young men. First to enter was a short, husky man, dressed in the uniform of an Israeli army paratroop captain. Behind him came another officer and a young Jew in civilian clothes, with a briefcase beneath his arm.

Elaborate greetings, in the flowery style of the Arabs, were exchanged. The captain shook hands with each man and motioned them to sit down. He remained standing, his chest adorned with ribbons denoting earlier battles against the Arabs, and began to speak. His Arabic was fluent, as was that of the other two Israelis with him.

Addressing himself to the elderly sheik, the captain said how happy he was to be once more in the mayor's majlis. He wished to remind the sheik that if any village problems arose the captain's office in nearby Ramallah always was open to the mayor. Then the captain grew brisk.

Introducing the young civilian with him, the officer said they had come to explain new taxation forms, developed by the Israeli occupation authorities for towns on the West Bank. The captain sat down, and the Jewish civilian took over.

First he held up a book of Jordanian law. Everything in the new form, he explained to the sheik and his village notables, was in accordance with "their own law," the law of the Hashemite Kingdom of Jordan. The Israelis were not trying to impose Jewish law on the town. Rather, they hoped to make it simpler for the sheik and for leaders of other Arab villages on the West Bank to collect municipal taxes, account for them, and decide for what purposes to use them.

Then the Jewish official handed a copy of the new taxation forms to each Arab present. The forms, printed in Arabic and Hebrew, were studied intently by most of the council members, as the Arabic-speaking Israeli described each item. The sheik nodded sagely from time to time, but it was clear that the young Arab at his side, busy writing notes as the Israeli talked, would have primary responsibility for implementing the new regulations.

The Israeli finished his explanation and sat down. Then he added a footnote. The neighboring village, he said casually, had just received a loan from the Israeli government for bringing electricity into the town. Should the sheik have a similar request to make, the Israelis would be happy to consider it.

Now the captain thanked the sheik for the courtesy of his reception, shook hands all around, and roared off in his jeep to the next town. Later the captain told me that he was responsible for the administration of ninety-three West Bank villages and three Bedouin tribes. He and the two men with him were in their twenties.

During the meeting Turkish coffee had been served in the ceremonial Arab way, and the young Jewish captain had refused to drink until the elderly sheik had been served. Nonetheless, there was no doubt who had been in charge during that session in the majlis. It was the Israeli captain, not the Arab mayor.

For the first time in its history that town, built on the slope of a stony hill on the Samarian heights, might have electricity to light its dusty streets and buildings of cut stone. Already the village had running water, brought in by the Israelis. The town, in other words, would be better off, if and when it went back to Arab control, than it had been when the Jewish occupation began.

But the captain had no illusions how the Arabs in that room felt about Jews. "When I first started this work," he remarked, "that particular sheik and his people were openly hostile. Now they are not." He shrugged. "They benefit from what we are doing."

The relationship, however, was awkward and artificial. The Israelis might be benevolent, but, in Arab eyes, they were conquerors who had taken away Arab lands and rights. I was reminded of the words of Maron Ben-Venisti, the Israeli in charge of East Jerusalem affairs: "We [Arabs and Jews] do not explore each other's thinking. . . . Sometimes it is better not to know exactly what the other one is thinking."

Defense Minister Moshe Dayan, himself an Arabic-speaking sabra, defined Arab attitudes in a talk before American businessmen in Tel Aviv in 1969.

Arab refugees wait to make the difficult crossing from the West Bank of the Jordan River across the King Hussein Bridge (formerly Allenby Bridge) into Jordan. (United Nations)

Why do the Arabs hate the Jews? Answer: They take us to be foreigners, invaders that took an Arab country and turned it into a Jewish state. And they are right about it. From their point of view, we did it. We didn't come here to contribute, or for a contribution to the Arab countries. We came here to establish our State because we feel that this is our homeland.

Dayan thus touched upon an issue that troubles many persons in the world. Few doubt the right of the Jewish people to have a homeland of their own. But was it necessary, in the process, to uproot and make homeless another people, namely the Arabs of Palestine? A majority of Palestinian Arabs, whose roots in the country lie centuries deep, now are expelled from their homeland with little hope of returning.

Many of these refugees live in makeshift camps, in tents or simple huts of concrete and tin, exposed to the winds of winter and the harsh summer sun. Lebanon, its population and governmental structure delicately balanced between Christians and Moslems, declines to give its Palestine Arabs citizenship, lest the scales be tipped in favor of the Moslems. Jordan granted citizenship to its refugees but can give few of them work, because the country is so poor. Hundreds of thousands of Arabs huddle jobless in the Gaza Strip. Egypt's long, narrow Nile valley, hemmed in by the desert on either side, is densely overpopulated as it is.

Iraq and Syria potentially could take many refugees and create work for them on land that is now lying fallow. For political reasons, however, these two states have accepted relatively few refugees. Iraq in particular has taken only a few thousand Palestine Arabs with special skills.

Almost all the annual budget of the United Nations Relief and Works Agency (UNRWA), to which the American government contributes more than half, is spent on basic food, clothing, and shelter for more than one million Arabs on refugee lists. Little is left over to train young men and women in skills that might enable them to break out of camp life and earn a living. In such

Scenes of Jewish life in a tapestry after a painting by Marc Chagall. The tapestry hangs in the Knesset.

an atmosphere of hopelessness and enervation, the Arab commando movement was spawned.

Divided into many different groups, the commandos have one common aim—to eliminate the State of Israel and restore Palestine to the Arabs. Terrorist raids into Israel from bases in Lebanon, Syria, and Jordan draw Israeli army reprisals. In 1970 the commandos alienated much of world opinion by throwing bombs at Israeli installations in Europe and by hijacking civil aircraft and holding innocent people hostage.

Arab governments, as we have noted, are caught in the middle. They hesitate to speak out openly against the terrorist tactics of the commandos, who represent, after all, the Palestinians who lost their homes. Yet responsible Arab leaders know that the commandos, while largely ineffective against Israel, harm the Arab image throughout the world. It remains to be seen, in any case, whether the commando units can regroup successfully, following their decisive defeat by King Hussein's Jordanian army in the summer of 1971.

Israelis see their return to Palestine from another point of view—that of a long-suffering people, forced centuries ago into exile, subject to discrimination, subtle or virulent. Only a homeland of their own, open to all the Jews of the world, can provide the Jewish people with an escape from potential persecution. That land, in the Zionist view, must be Palestine, where the Jewish nation had its beginning under Abraham, Moses, David, and the prophets, thousands of years ago.

Many more Jews live outside Israel than in the Zionist state. Jews of the United States, Britain, France, and other western lands are free to move to Israel if they wish. For the most part this is not true of the 2,485,000 Jews of the Soviet Union, nor of thousands more in other Communist lands and in Arab countries. Israelis feel primary allegiance not to the uprooted Arabs of Palestine, but to those Jewish brethren who still long in vain for the promised land.

The tragedy is that two Semitic peoples, not one, regard Palestine as their rightful home.

Books for Further Reading

ACKROYD, PETER R., *Israel Under Babylon and Persia*. New York, Oxford University Press, 1970.

APPEL, BENJAMIN, *Ben-Gurion's Israel*. New York, Grosset & Dunlap, Inc., 1965.

AVNERY, URI, *Israel Without Zionists: A Plea for Peace in the Middle East*. New York, The Macmillan Company, 1968.

BEN-GURION, DAVID, *Israel: A Personal History*. New York, Thomas Y. Crowell Company, Inc. (Funk & Wagnalls/ Sabra Book), 1971.

—— *Israel, Years of Challenge*. New York, Holt, Rinehart and Winston, Inc., 1963.

BRILLIANT, MOSHE, *Portrait of Israel*. New York, American Heritage Press, 1970.

BUBER, MARTIN, *Israel and the World: Essays in a Time of Crisis*. New York, Schocken Books, Inc., 1948.

BURDETT, WINSTON, *Encounter With the Middle East: An Intimate Report on What Lies Behind the Arab-Israeli Conflict*. New York, Atheneum Publishers, 1969.

COHEN, ABNER, *Arab Border Villages in Israel*. New York, Humanities Press, Inc., 1965.

COHEN, AHARON, *Israel and the Arab World*. New York, Funk & Wagnalls Company, Inc., 1970.

COMAY, JOAN, *Ben-Gurion and the Birth of Israel*. New York, Random House, Inc., 1967.

COOLIDGE, OLIVIA, *People in Palestine*. New York, Houghton Mifflin Company, 1965.

DINUR, BEN Z., *Israel and the Diaspora*. Philadelphia, Jewish Publication Society of America, 1969.

DRAPER, THEODORE, *Israel and World Politics: Roots of the Third Arab-Israeli War*. New York, The Viking Press, 1968.

EDELMAN, LILY, *Israel: New People in an Old Land*, rev. ed. New York, Thomas Nelson, Inc., 1968.

ELLIS, HARRY B., *The Arabs* (Major Cultures of the World series). Cleveland and New York, The World Publishing Company, 1958.

ELON, AMOS, *The Israelis: Founders and Sons*. New York, Holt, Rinehart and Winston, Inc., 1971.

ESSRIG, HARRY, and SEGAL, ABRAHAM, *Israel Today*, rev. ed. New York, Union of American Hebrew Congregations, 1968.

FEIGENBAUM, LAWRENCE, and SEIGEL, KALMAN, *Israel: Crossroads of Conflict*. New York, Rand McNally & Company, 1968.

HIRSCHFELD, BURT, *A State Is Born, The Story of Israel*. New York, Julian Messner, Inc., 1967.

HOFFMAN, GAIL, *Land and People of Israel* (Portraits of the Nation series), rev. ed. Philadelphia, J. B. Lippincott Company, 1963.

HOLISHER, DESIDER, *Growing Up in Israel*. New York, The Viking Press, 1963.

KOSUT, HAL, *Israel and the Arabs: The June 1967 War*. New York, Facts on File, Inc., 1968.

LANDAU, JACOB M. *Arabs in Israel: A Political Study*. New York, Oxford University Press, 1969.

MEEKER, ODIN, *Israel: Ancient Land, Young Nation.* New York, Charles Scribner's Sons, 1968.

PRITTIE, TERENCE C. *Miracle in the Desert,* rev. ed. Baltimore, Penguin Books, Inc., 1968.

RACHLEFF, OWEN S., *Young Israel: A History of the Modern Nation.* New York, Lion Press, 1968.

RODINSON, MAXIME, *Israel and the Arabs,* trans. by Michael Perl. Baltimore, Penguin Books, Inc., 1970.

SACHAR, HOWARD M., *From the Ends of the Earth, The People of Israel.* New York, Dell Publishing Company, Inc., 1970.

SAFRAN, NADAV, *From War to War: The Arab-Israeli Confrontation.* New York, Pegasus (Western Pub. Co., Inc.), 1969.

TUCHMAN, BARBARA W., *The Bible and the Sword: England and Palestine from the Bronze Age to Balfour.* New York, Funk & Wagnalls Company, Inc., 1968.

Index

Abdullah, King, 41, 65, 66, 73, 81, 84, 92
Abraham, 3, 13-17, 20, 21, 22, 25, 81, 89, 173
Adenauer, Konrad, 123-124
Agudat Israel, 113
Alexander of Macedon, 26
Alexander II, Czar, 30
Al Fatah, 84
Algeria, 82, 83, 128, 142, 145
Aliyas, 43, 50
Allah, 22, 23
Allied Peace Conference (San Remo), 41
Allon, Yigal, 133
American Jewish Congress, 164
American University of Beirut, 95, 149-150, 164
American University of Cairo, 149-150, 164
American Zionist Organization, 56

anti-Semitism, 31-32, 142
Arab commando movement, 84-86, 102, 141, 145, 172-173
Arab Executive, 53
Arab Higher Committee, 54
Arabia, 13, 22, 79
Arab-Israeli war of 1967, see Six-Day War
Arab Jewish war of 1948, 7, 23, 61-65, 153
Arab-Jewish war of 1956, 67-69, 146, 154
Arab League, 83, 164
Arab Legion of Transjordan, 64, 90
Arab Rebellion (1936-1939), 54, 82
Arab Republic of Egypt (see also Egypt), 84
Arabs:
  armies of, 61, 84-85
  and British, 37-39, 52-55, 80

Arabs (*cont.*)
  federation attempts of, 80-81,
    84-86
  under Israel, 92-100, 103, 136-
    141, 167-171
  in mandate period, 52-59
  modernization among, 94-98,
    168-169
  nations of, and Israel, 79-87,
    100-101, 157-164
  origins and history of, 21-23,
    27-28, 79-80
  refugee problem of, 63, 64, 65-
    66, 75, 84, 94, 101-103, 152,
    170, 171-172
  territory of, occupied by Israel,
    73-76, 88-101, 157-161
  and UN, 59, 158-160
  and U.S., 40, 59, 142, 149-165
Arad, Gen. Yizhak, 108-111
Arafat, Yasir, 84-85
Artaxerxes I, King of Persia, 25
Assembly (mandate period), 51,
  52

Babylon, 16, 20, 25
Baghdad Pact, 153-154
balance of payments, 122-123,
  131
Balfour, Arthur James, 35, 36,
  41
Balfour Declaration, 36-37
Bedouins, 23, 39, 41, 61, 137-138,
  139, 169
Begin, Menahem, 64, 134
Ben-Gurion, David, 52, 56, 156
Ben-Venisti, Maron, 90-92, 98,
  99-100, 169
Bernadotte, Count Folke, 63, 64
Bethlehem, 16, 54, 98
Biltmore Program, 56
Black Panthers (oriental Jews),
  111, 112

Boumedienne, Houari, 83
Bourguiba, Habib, 83
Bull, Gen. Odd, 73
Byzantines, 27

Cabinet, Israeli, 135, 136
Canaan, 16, 17
chaverim, 45-50
Choveve Zion, 33-34
Christians, Christianity, 22, 27,
  31, 171
Churchill, Winston, 35
Cohen, Haim, 117
Columbus, Christopher, 28
Communist parties, 133, 134, 137
Constantinople, 27
Constantinople Convention
  (1888), 69-70
contributions, from world Jewry,
  123, 124, 151
Crusaders, 23, 27, 28
Cyrus the Great, 25, 26

Dair Yasin massacre, 63, 64
Damascus, 38, 39, 79, 80, 81, 83
  Arab meeting (1920) in, 41
David, King, 19, 22, 135, 173
  tomb of, 33
Dayan, Moshe, 49, 85-86, 133,
  169-171
Dead Sea, 3-4
Degania, 49
de Gaulle, Charles, 128
Diaspora, 28-31, 34, 114, 119
divorce, 115-116
Dulles, John Foster, 153-154
Druze, the, 138, 140-141

Eastern Orthodox church, 27
East Jerusalem, *see* Jerusalem
Eban, Abba, 133
Eddy, Col. William A., 150
education, 44-45, 51, 108-111

Egypt (*see also* United Arab Republic), 17-18, 59, 61, 63, 67, 80-81, 82, 105, 131
  occupied territories of, 75-76, 100-101, 157
  pharaohs of, 17-18
  and Soviet Union, 71, 142-146, 154, 156
  and Suez Canal, 68, 69-71, 82-83, 101, 144, 145, 154, 161
  and U.S., 142, 149, 150, 153-155, 163-164
  in war of 1956, 68-69, 153
Eilat, port of, 69, 74, 100
Eisenhower, Dwight D., 69, 86, 153, 157, 160
European Economic Community (EEC), 84, 127-128
Ezra the Scribe, 25

family life, 44-46, 50
Farouk, King, 67
fedayeen, 67, 80, 84
Federation of Arab Republics, 84
Feisal, King of Saudi Arabia, 81, 82
Feisal, King of Syria and Iraq, 39-40, 41, 52, 65, 81
Feisal II, King of Iraq, 81
fellahin, 61, 72
Ferdinand and Isabella, 28
France, 134, 173
  and Israel, 128
  and Middle East, 37-38, 41, 80, 128, 149, 152, 162
  in war of 1956, 68
Frankfurter, Felix, 39-40

Gahal, 135
Galilee, 19, 63
Gaza, 67, 72, 160
Gaza Strip, 67, 69, 74, 75, 76, 84, 100, 146, 153, 171

General Council (mandate period), 51
General Federation of Labor, *see* Histadrut
George, David Lloyd, 35
Germany (*see also* West Germany), 39
  Jews in, 10, 28, 54, 124
ghettos, 28-29
Golan Heights, 66, 71, 73, 74, 76, 81, 101
Goliath, 19
Gordon, Aaron David, 44, 49
Great Britain, 23, 28, 43, 106, 107-108, 116, 134, 152, 162, 173
  and Arabs, 37-39, 52-55, 81, 149
  in mandate period, 50-59
  in war of 1956, 68
  and Zionists, 35-37, 51, 53-54, 55, 56-57
Greater Syria (*see also* Syria), 84
Greece, 128, 151
guerrilla warfare, 61-63, 66, 85-86

Haganah, 54, 61-63, 142
Hagar, 17, 21
Haifa, 5, 7, 52, 92, 93
Haifa clause, 163
Haj Amin el Husseini, 52
Hall, Paul, 163-164
Hammarskjold, Dag, 69, 70
Hashemite family, 37, 38, 41
Hashemite Kingdom of Jordan (*see also* Jordan), 41, 65, 92, 168
Hassan, King of Morocco, 83
Hausner, Gideon, 108, 114-116
Hebrews (*see also* Jews):
  origins of, 13-17
  under Moses, 17-18
  twelve tribes of, 19-20

Hebrew University, 51, 94
Henry II, King of Castile, 28
Herut, 134-135
Herzl, Theodor, 34-35
Histadrut, 51, 52, 112, 128-130, 137
Hitler, Adolf, 54, 55, 123, 124
Holland, Jews in, 28, 29
Hussein, King of Jordan, 66, 73, 81, 85, 86, 97, 100, 101, 135, 155, 156, 173
Hussein, Sharif, 37-38, 39, 82

Ibn Saud, Abdul Aziz, 81-82
Iran, 26, 69, 84, 154
Iraq, 16, 37, 38, 41, 59, 71, 81, 84, 100, 105, 142, 145, 154, 171
Irgun Zvai Leumi, 56-57, 63, 64, 134
Isaac, 3, 17, 21, 89
Ishmael, 17, 21
Islam, 27, 79
    background of, 22-23
Israel, State of:
    agriculture in, 5, 44, 47, 50, 51, 95-96
    Arabs in, 76-77, 90-100, 136-141
    and Arab states, 79-87, 100-101, 157-164
    boycott of, 83-84, 162-164
    church and state in, 112-119, 137
    cultural conflict in, 105-112
    establishment of, 52, 59, 63, 151
    government in, 135-136
    immigration to, 102-103, 105-112, 121, 125, 146-147
    and Soviet Union, 141-142, 146-147
    trade routes of, 69, 71, 83-84

Israel, State of (cont.)
    and UN, 59, 64, 66, 68, 75-76, 101
Israeli army, 49, 66, 138-141
    education in, 108-111
Israel Labor Party, 133, 134

Jacob (Israel), 17
Jarring, Gunnar, 158
Jehovah, 20
Jericho, 18, 19
Jerusalem, 4, 19-20, 52, 54, 81, 93, 137
    in Arab-Jewish conflict, 97-99
    Jewish Quarter of, 89-90, 94
    Old City of (East Jerusalem), 3, 23, 74, 76, 87-92, 93, 98, 100, 101-102
    rulers of, 25-27
Jesus, 22, 27
Jewish Agency, 51, 52, 55
Jewish Brigade Group, 56
Jewish Colonial Trust, 34
Jewish National Fund, 34, 51, 53
Jews:
    assimilation of, 31, 33, 37, 44, 55
    early history of, 13-21, 25-27
    exile and dispersion of, 20-21, 28-31
    immigration of, 30-31, 43-44, 50-51, 53, 54, 55-56, 102-103, 105-112, 121, 125, 146-147
    in mandate period, 50-59
    oriental vs. western origins of, 105-112
    persecution of, 28-31, 54, 55-56
    in Soviet Union, 146-147, 173
Johnson, Lyndon B., 154, 157-158
Johnston, Eric, 86, 87

Jordan, 1, 7, 49, 81, 83, 84, 86, 135, 155, 171
  guerrillas based in, 8, 66, 67, 84, 85, 100, 141, 172
  occupied territories of, 73-75, 88-100, 101, 157
  in war of 1967, 73-75
Jordan River (*see also* West Bank), 4, 65, 74, 86-87, 135
Jordan River valley, 6, 18, 38
Joseph, 17
Joshua, 18
Judah, 18-19
Judaism, and Jewishness, 112-113, 117-119
Judea, 26

Kennedy, John F., 154, 155, 156-157
kibbutzim, 10, 11, 44-50, 51, 53, 54, 121, 130
King, Henry C., 40
Knesset, 52, 64, 90, 98, 102-103, 108, 113, 115, 116, 118, 129, 133, 135, 136, 137
Kollek, Teddy, 90, 99
Koran, 22
Kuwait, 82, 83, 152

Law of Return, 102-103, 106, 118
Lawrence, T. E., 37
League of Nations, 55
Lebanon, 1, 6, 37, 38, 40, 41, 59, 84, 86, 100, 140, 172
  factions in, 80, 171
Liberal Party, Israel, 134, 135
Libya, 82-83, 84
Luxembourg Agreement, 123-124

Maccabean Revolt, 21, 26
Maccabeus, Judas, 26-27
MacDonald, Ramsay, 53-54
McMahon, Sir Henry, 38

Maki faction, 134
mandate period, 50-59
manufacturing, 47, 48
Mapam, 134, 137
Marcus School, 109-110
Masada, fortress of, 26
Mecca, 22, 89
Meir, Golda, 118, 133, 160
Mesopotamia, 16, 20, 26, 81
Mixed Armistice Commissions, 65
Mohammed, 3, 13, 22, 23, 89
monotheism, 20, 22
Morocco, 82, 83, 105
Moses, 17-18, 20, 22, 25, 114, 117
moshavim, 50, 51
Moslem courts, 116-117, 137
Moslems (*see also* Islam), 79-80, 89, 116
Mosque of Omar, 23, 89
Mount Carmel, 5, 109
Mount Moriah, 89
Mount Zion, 33
Moyne, Lord, 57

Nasser, Gamal Abdel, 67, 68, 69-70, 71, 72, 73, 80-81, 82, 100, 142, 143, 144, 153, 154, 155, 159-160
National Religious Party, 113, 116, 134
Naturei Karta, 113
Nazareth, 6, 8
Nazis, 10, 28, 54, 55, 123-124, 150
Nebuchadnezzar, 20, 25
Negev, 3, 4, 20, 63, 69, 86-87, 137-138
Nehemiah, 25
Nimeiry, Gen. Gaafar al-, 144
Nir Eliahu, 6-11
Nissim, Yitzhak, 118
Nixon, Richard M., 134, 159, 162
North Atlantic Treaty, 160

oil, 69, 82, 83, 84, 130-131, 151, 152-153, 155
Ottoman Turks, *see* Turks

Pale of Settlement, in Russia, 29-30
Palestine (*see also* Israel):
    under Arabs, 23
    British role in, 23, 28, 37-39, 43, 50, 52, 53-57
    geography of, 1-7
    immigration to, 43-44, 50-51, 53, 54, 55-56, 58
    Jewish commitment to, 16-17
    mandate period in, 50-59
    non-Jewish rule in, 25-28
    partition of, 54, 57-59, 62, 63, 64, 103, 142, 151
    population shifts in, 50-51, 76
    as promised land, 21, 34-35, 49, 77, 81
    after World War I, 40-41, 149
Palestine Arab Congress, 53
Palestinian Arabs, 50, 52-59, 64, 65-66, 75, 76, 84-85, 136-141, 167-173
Pan-Arabism, 40, 79
Paris peace conference, 39
Persian empire, 25-26
Philistines, 19, 27
Podgorny, Nikolai, 145-146
pogroms, 29-30
Poland, Jews in, 31, 53
Pompidou, Georges, 128
Ptolemies of Egypt, 26

Qalqilya, 6-11, 65, 66
Qibya, Israeli raid on, 66

Rakah faction, 134, 137
Rogers, William P., 159, 161
Roman Catholic Church, 28
Rothschild, Baron Edmond de, 43

Rufeisin, Oswald, 117
Russia (*see also* Soviet Union):
    emigration from, 29-31, 43-44
    Zionism in, 33-34, 49

sabras, 108, 111, 112
Sadat, Anwar el-, 100, 144, 146, 161
Saladin, 27
Sarah, 17, 21
Saudi Arabia, 59, 61, 81-82, 83, 150, 152, 155, 162-163, 164
Seafarers International Union, 163-164
Shalit, Benjamin, 117-118
Shapiro, Yakov S., 102
Sharef, Zev, 98
Sharett, Moshe, 123, 124
Sharm el-Sheikh, 69, 71, 74, 75, 100, 160
Shefer, Eliezer, 125
Sinai Peninsula, 1, 18, 20, 38, 49, 76, 100, 101, 130, 131, 146, 161
    campaign of 1956 in, 68, 69, 153
    in war of 1967, 71, 72, 75
Six-Day War, 10, 49, 71-76, 84, 102, 112, 121, 128, 136, 145, 157-158
socialism, 133-134
social welfare, 130, 134
Solomon, King, 22, 89, 135
Soviet-Egyptian Treaty, 145-146
Soviet Union, 13, 59, 68, 106
    and the Middle East, 67, 71, 141-147, 153-154, 156, 162
    weapons supplied by, 71, 72, 142, 143, 145, 146, 156
Stern Gang, 56-57, 63
Strait of Tiran, 69, 71, 83, 84, 100, 101, 160
Sudan, 83, 84, 144, 145
Suez Canal, 68, 69-71, 72, 83, 101,

Suez Canal (*cont.*)
131, 143, 144, 145, 154, 159, 160, 161
Sykes-Picot Agreement, 37-38, 41
Syria, 1, 26, 27, 37, 38, 40, 41, 49, 59, 71, 85, 86, 100, 140, 145, 149, 171
  attacks by, 66, 81
  occupied land of, 75-76, 101
  in U.A.R., 80-81, 84
  in war of 1967, 73, 81

taxes, 121-122, 125
Tel Aviv, 5, 6, 52, 142, 146, 169
Temple of Solomon, 20, 89
terrorists:
  Arabs as, 9, 54, 66, 172
  Jews as, 56-57, 63-64
Tigris and Euphrates, 13-16, 20
Transjordan (*see also* Jordan), 41, 59, 64
Tripartite Declaration of 1950, 152, 160
Truman, Harry S., 150, 153, 154, 160
Tunisia, 82, 83
Turkey, 27, 128, 154
Turks, 23, 27, 37, 38, 39, 79-80

United Arab Republic (*see also* Egypt), 1, 80-81, 82, 83, 84, 142-146
United Nations, 13, 68, 75-76, 101, 158
  partition of Palestine by, 57-59, 62, 63, 64, 103, 142, 151
  peacekeeping operations of, 65, 66-67, 69, 71, 73, 159-160
United Nations Emergency Force (UNEF), 69, 71, 72
United Nations Relief and Works

UNRWA (*cont.*)
  Agency (UNRWA), 65-66, 75, 171
United Nations Special Committee on Palestine (UNSCOP), 57-59, 64
United Nations Truce Supervision Organization (UNTSO), 65
United States, 13, 44, 59, 81, 106, 121, 122, 134, 135, 142, 173
  and Israel, 84, 86, 98, 149-165
  Zionists in, 39, 40, 56, 150-151, 161
U Thant, 158

Wailing Wall, 87-89
Wandervögel, 49
Weizmann, Chaim, 35-36, 39, 40, 52, 53, 65
West Bank, 73, 76, 81, 88, 101
  Arab-Jewish relations in, 92-100, 103, 141, 167-170
West Germany, 127, 134
  aid to Israel by, 123-124, 125
White Paper, 53-56
Wilson, Woodrow, 40, 149-150
Wingate, Orde, 54
World War I, 35, 36, 37, 38-39
World War II, 10, 35, 55-57
World Zionist Organization, 34-35, 43, 51, 52

Yemen, 82, 105, 106, 146

Zionism, Zionists:
  British and, 35-37, 51, 53-54, 55, 56-57
  Judaism and, 112-119
  land-buying of, 34, 51-53, 55
  land settlement, 43-50
  origins of, 32-35, 112, 173
  and UN, 59

About the Author

Harry B. Ellis, journalist, author, and lecturer, has traveled widely throughout Israel, the Arab world from Morocco to Iraq, and all parts of Europe. Formerly chief of the Paris Bureau of *The Christian Science Monitor*, he is now staff correspondent for this newspaper in Bonn, West Germany. He also does radio reporting for the Columbia Broadcasting System from Europe. Mr. Ellis has written many books for both adults and young people on topics ranging from the Middle East to his most recent *Ideals and Ideologies: Communism, Socialism, and Capitalism*. He has also lectured widely in the United States on foreign affairs. In 1959 Mr. Ellis was awarded the degree of Honorary Doctor of Humane Letters by Wesleyan University for his writings on the Middle East. He currently lives with his family in Bonn.